SCHOOL CURRICULUM AND TEACHING

Books by **Marlow Ediger**
& Digumarti Bhaskara Rao

Administration of Schools
Community Colleges
Curriculum Organisation
Curriculum of School Subjects
Curriculum, School and Teacher
Effective Schooling
Effective School Curriculum
Elementary Curriculum
Elementary Curriculum Improvement
Essays on School Curriculum
Essays on School Issues
Essays on Teaching Mathematics
Essays on Teaching Science
Essays on Teaching Social Studies
Essays on Teaching Reading
Essays on Teaching and Learning
Improving School Administration
Issues in School Curriculum
Language Arts Curriculum
Philosophy and Curriculum
Psychology and Curriculum
Quality School Education
Reading Curriculum and Instruction
Relevancy in Elementary Curriculum
School Organisation
School Curriculum and Administration
School Curriculum and TEACHING
Science Curriculum
Teaching English Successfully
Teaching Language Arts Successfully
Teaching Mathematics Successfully
Teaching Science Successfully
Teaching Social Studies Successfully
Teaching Mathematics in Elementary Schools
Teaching Science in Elementary Schools
Successful School Administration
Successful School Education

SCHOOL CURRICULUM AND TEACHING

By

Prof. Marlow Ediger

M.A., B.S.E., Ed.D.

Emeritus Professor of Education

Truman State University

201 West 22nd Street

North Newton KS 67117

United States of America

&

Prof. Digumarti Bhaskara Rao

M.Sc., M.A., M.A., M.Ed., Ph.D.

Principal

R.V.R. College of Education

D-43 (277) S.V.N. Colony

Guntur - 522 006 (India)

&

Member

Board of Studies in Education

Acharya Nagarjuna University

Nagarjuna Nagar - 522 510 (India)

DISCOVERY PUBLISHING HOUSE PVT. LTD.

NEW DELHI-110 002

Published by:
Tilak Wasan

DISCOVERY PUBLISHING HOUSE PVT. LTD.
4383/4B, Ansari Road, Darya Ganj
New Delhi-110 002 (India)
Phone : +91-11-23279245, 43596064-65
Fax : +91-11-23253475
E-mail : discoverypublishinghouse@gmail.com
sales@discoverypublishinggroup.com
parul.wasan@gmail.com
web : www.discoverypublishinggroup.com

***First Edition:* 2014**

ISBN: 978-93-5056-432-5

School Curriculum and Teaching

Printed at:
Dynamic Printers
Delhi

Dedicated
to

SARAT, HARSHITHA, SRIVEDA
Vancouver, Canada

Preface

School is an institution designed for the teaching of students under the direction of teachers. The primary school is meant for young children and secondary school is for teenagers who have completed their primary education.

Curriculum is prescriptive and is based on a more general syllabus which merely specifies what topics must be understood and to what level to achieve a particular grade or standard. It is also a prescribed course of studies, which students must fulfill in order to pass a certain level of education.

Teaching is the facilitation of another's learning. They direct the education of students and might draw on many school subjects like languages, mathematics, science and social studies as they form mandatory subjects in school learning.

Several issues concerned to school curriculum and teaching are discussed in this book. This book will be of great use to the curriculum designers, textbook authors, teachers and administrators.

Digumarti Bhaskara Rao

Sri Sai Soudha
D-43 S.V.N.
Guntur-522006
India

Contents

Issues in the School Curriculum

There are a plethora of issues in curriculum development which need resolving. These issues reveal diverse philosophies and psychologies of learning. Each side has merits as well as problems. Then too, perhaps, one side of an issue will be more appealing to an intellect than the other; this will be especially true in a democracy where diversity is prized in ideas presented. A brief analysis of each issue will be given.

An Analysis of Curricular Issues

There, no doubt, will be more issues than those presented in this writing. First, charter schools tend to be increasing greatly in number. When charters were first implemented, the emphasis was that these schools be innovative and free from unnecessary rules and regulations which govern the public schools. It almost sounded as if charters were to be experimental in nature. New ideas in teaching might then be tried out and publicized. The calls for accountability will make for a more uniform curriculum with that of the regular public schools. Accountability stresses testing to notice how well pupils are doing in achievement when progress is compared among and between individual school systems and states in the nation. Accountability, also, holds teachers responsible for pupil progress, based on test score results. For their operation, charter schools siphon moneys from public schools. There are several questions pertaining to charter schools:

- How is pupil performance appraised in charter schools when making comparisons with those in the public schools?
- Does money taken from public schools to run charters hinder pupil achievement in the former?
- Has charter schools truly made for quality innovative procedures in teaching?
- If doing away with selected regulations for charters help learner achievement, why not do away with these same regulations in the public schools? (Ediger 2008).

Second, mandated testing to indicate pupil progress emphasizes sameness (standardization) in test items for all pupils on a particular grade level, sameness in time limits for all in test taking, sameness in directions for taking the test, among other facets of uniformity. "One size fits all," is a slogan to be used here: however, pupils differ from each in many ways such as ability, interests, and purposes, among other ways.

Teachers, here, may have written objectives to use as guidelines for teaching and learning situations. The objectives are the same for each grade level. Teachers need to teach and pupils need to learn what is in the objectives in order to pass the standardized, mandated test. Pupils may experience much drill, prior to test taking.

Toward the other end of the continuum is constructivism, a philosophy/psychology of instruction which stresses no drill and no mandated testing of pupils. Responsibility for learning resides with the individual learner. The teacher motivates, encourages, challenges, and facilitates achievement. Pupils are active participants in learning, not passive recipients of knowledge and skills. Lecture as a method of teaching is not emphasized; instead, learning by discovery is stressed. Here, pupils are guided to develop their very own concepts and generalizations. If a pupil has a question in an ongoing lesson, he/she is assisted through teacher questioning to arrive at a correct answer. If opinions are involved, pupils individually are to develop their own conclusions, based on knowledge, rational thought and decision making. It is the pupil who must do the learning and not the teacher. The teacher's role is to assist pupils to secure needed answers. Pupil ownership of the curriculum is important. In this way, constructivists believe that pupils optimize learning when it is self directed (See Alam, 2009).

Pupils sequence their very own learnings when content is not understood; assistance from teachers in these teaching and learning situations makes for order in meaningful contextual situations. Building upon past learning experiences aids the pupil in bringing order to what is being acquired.

Third, selected educators believe in strict emphasis upon the academics in the school setting. Focusing on subject matter content in the curriculum receives priority. Basal textbooks are utilized to provide major learnings for pupils. Objectives in the curriculum, for example, reflect the importance of the social sciences (history, geography, economics and political science), mathematics (arithmetic, algebra, geometry, among others), English and the natural sciences (biology, physics, chemistry, as well as the earth sciences). Art, music and physical education are somewhat peripheral, Educators focusing upon the academics believe the academics provide a quality basis for general education in pursing further vocational, professional and career ends. Mandated state objectives for pupil attainment presently emphasize content from the academics (See Fitzhugh, 2006).

Toward the other end of the curriculum, an activity centered curriculum is stressed. Here, a more open ended curriculum is being stressed to meet individual pupil needs. Thus, pupil/teacher planning may be emphasized. Thus within an ongoing unit of study, pupils individually or collectively identify a problem. The problem requires deliberation and thought, not factual answers. Indepth learning from a variety of references sources are utilized to secure a tentative answer, resulting in an hypothesis. The hypothesis is subject to testing, and as a result, may be modified or refuted. New problems might well arise in these endeavors (See Ford, 2008).

The role of the teacher in problem solving activities encompasses being a guide, a resource person and a motivator. The teacher does not lecture but, rather, helps pupils to locate necessary information to solve identified problems. With problem solving, pupils are:

- actively engaged in learning and not being passive recipients of knowledge and skills.
- ordering their own experiences and not following the dictates of the teacher.
- moving around in the classroom to locate reference sources of information.
- motivated by peers as well as the teacher in ongoing endeavors (Dewey, 1916).

Fourth, teaching toward having pupils achieve specific objectives is advocated by behaviourists as a psychology of learning. The objectives must be clearly stated so there is no guesswork as to what pupils are to learn. The objectives are stated prior to instruction and leave little/no leeway for flexibility. Learning activities are carefully aligned with the objectives so that each objective might be achieved by learners. Evaluation stresses if pupils did/did not achieve the objective being emphasized. Each of three components of the curriculum-objectives, learning opportunities, and evaluation procedures is closely structured and related.

Toward the other end of the continuum, a multi-media curriculum might be implemented for pupils to attain a flexible number of objectives. A variety of concrete, semi-concrete, and abstract experiences may be provided to stress in making provision for individual differences. These activities provide for different learning styles possessed by pupils. Thus, pupils may benefit from the learning opportunity which harmonizes best with an individual style of learning. Self-evaluation by pupils may be used to ascertain achievement and progress. The teacher also uses diverse evaluation techniques including teacher observation along with teacher written tests to ascertain how well pupils are learning.

Fifth, selected educators emphasize the basics in the curriculum for all pupils to take as course work. Pupil achievement is considered important in mastering essential knowledge and skills. The basics represent a core of ideas which pupils must possess in order to do well in society. Abstract concepts and generalizations, coming from the basics, provide objectives for learner attainment. Advocates of the basics in the curriculum believe that core knowledge and skills are the best approach in preparing individuals for future occupations, jobs and professions (Ediger, 2008).

To achieve essential subject matter, pupils need to experience selected content appropriate for sequential grade levels. Pupils need to be tested frequently to notice if the basics are being attained. These essentials can be identified and be tested upon in multiple choice test items on mandated tests.

Toward the other end of the continuum, pupils may choose from several options, as determined by the teacher, what to learn. Choices are involved and the learner is the decision maker as to what meets personal interests and purposes. They may also involve choosing between individual versus committee or collective endeavors. The pupil is to do the learning and must have an important role in making choices. If pupils can make decisions in terms of what to learn, they tend to make choices based on personal abilities and needs. Pupils achieve more optimally if they are actively involved in making selections in ongoing lessons and units of study, rather than being passive recipients of predetermined objectives to attain (Ediger, 2007).

Sixth, much of a pupil's school time is spent in the classroom, experiencing a basics curriculum or where choices are made in terms of what to learn and achieve. The former stresses more of what is to be accomplished in order to do well on mandated tests, while the latter philosophy is predicated on looking at the learner to ascertain meeting personal needs in the curriculum. Somewhat opposite, pupils may use the community to foster what is deemed useful in society for pupil learning. Resource personnel may then come into the classroom to talk about their specialty and use related AV aids in their presentation as it relates to a unit of study or a lesson. Pupils with teacher supervision may also visit a site in the community, relating it to previous learnings acquired. Real objectives from another culture may also be brought into a classroom and discussed. Learner questions need careful attention and may be used as follow ups to encourage project methods in subsequent activities. By relating the community to classroom experiences, pupils experience authenticity in learning. Using the community as a basis for learning may also be expanded with the following, among others:

- visits to nursing homes to present programs and interact with older people
- doing age appropriate, safe community service projects
- preparing/eating native food dishes as they relate to a selected culture being studied
- making bird houses and feeders to notice bird migration in the out of doors
- learning folk dances of another nation.

Seventh, technology is certainly seeing its many uses in teaching and learning situations. This includes online learning. There are baccalaureate, masters' and doctoral degrees offered by universities online. High school students are taking an increasing number of courses online. This, no doubt, will increase in number as kindergarten pupils are being introduced to working on the computer to solve math problems as well as to read library books thereon.

Online learning is very convenient to the student in that he/she may complete course work when convenient. When taking these courses at home, there is very little travel expense. Time is saved from traveling to a university campus and from traffic frustration that might well be spent in studying and completing courses. Quality needs to be insured in each course taken online. As is usually the case, there are also disadvantages:

- there is little time for interaction with the instructor and with peers
- virtual reality is emphasized and authenticity tends to be lacking
- the student must be well disciplined and motivated to pursue and complete online coursework.
- learning becomes highly abstract and lacks the concreteness, for example, of observing teachers at work.

More high quality research must be done to determine the effectiveness of online learning, as well as of each curriculum plan discussed.

REFERENCES

Alam, Mahmood (2009), "Academic Achievement in Relation to Creativity and Achievement Motivation; A Correlational Study," *Edutracks*, 8(9), 31-34.

Dewey, John (1916), *Democracy and Education*, New York: The Macmillan Company.

Ediger, Marlow (2007), "Teacher Observation to Assess Student Achievement," *Journal of Instructional Psychology*, 34 (3), 127-139.

Ediger, Marlow (2008), "Leadership in the School Setting," *Education*, 129(1), 17-20.

Ediger, Marlow (2008), "Modern School Mathematics," *College Student Journal*, 42 (4), 986-989.

Fitzhugh, Will (2006), "Where's the Content?" *Educational Leadership*, 64 (2), 42-47.

Ford, Dennis (2008), "Student Success the Way They Need It: Powerful School Change," *Phi delta Kappan*, 90 (4), 281-291.

Chapter 2 Issues in Curriculum Improvement

There are two somewhat opposing psychologies in education which have stood the test of time in the school curriculum. One psychology was developed largely by E. L. Thorndike (1874-1949) who emphasized *behaviorism* as a school of thought in developing the curriculum with his precise behaviorally stated objectives. These objectives must be stated, prior to instruction, for pupils to achieve. Aligned tests to measure progress reveal what pupils have learned. The teacher is largely in control of classroom activities.

Toward the other end of the curriculum, John Dewey (1859-1952) stressed *experimentalism*, as a philosophical school of thought, with problem solving being a key component. Considerable pupil involvement is then emphasized in teaching and learning situations (Ediger and Rao 2002).

Behaviorism Versus Experimentalism

Behaviorists believe strongly in the *measurement* concept with it strict emphasis upon obtaining numerical results from pupil achievement in terms of test scores. E. L. Thorndike advocated that "Anything which exists, exists in some amount, and if it exists in some amount, it can be measured." Thus, in any curriculum area, pupil progress can be measured to ascertain achievement. The following plans of testing emphasize behaviorism:

- mandated testing on the state level. The results are used to determine promotion of pupils to the next grade level, such as in grades three through eight and an exit test on the secondary level for graduation purposes.

- national tests to ascertain how well pupils are doing in achievement from year to year, such as the National Assessment of Educational Progress (NAEP).
- international tests to compare different nations in pupil achievement such as TIMSS (Third International Mathematics and Science Study) (See Griffen 2004).

Characteristics of behaviorism include the following:

- precision in test results are provided such as a pupil being on the sixtieth percentile, meaning out of every one hundred pupils tested, forty are above and 60 below the sixtieth percentile.
- teachers teaching toward pupils achieving specific, precise objectives.
- pupils receiving the same directions for test taking, the same length of time for each test taken and the same test items for the designated grade level of the test. Thus, all variables are the same, except for the pupils taking the test.
- multiple choice test items, generally, being on each test. These can be machine scored using the same answer key for each grade level test.
- print outs obtained from test results indicating the percentile, grade equivalent, stanine, or age equivalent of the test taker.
- test results also indicate which test items were missed. This provides a basis for review/new objectives for pupil attainment.

With behaviorism, there is a very close connection among objectives, learning activities and appraisal results. Cognitive objectives are the main stay of behaviorism. These objectives must be carefully sequenced so that pupil success is in the offing. Learning activities are focused upon pupils achieving the specific ends. Teachers need to be educated and trained to teach for pupils achieving the specific objectives, only. Evaluation stresses the importance of tests measuring what is contained in the precise objectives of instruction. Guess work is taken out of the equation with behaviorism as a psychology of instruction due to interaction among the objectives, learning activities and appraisal procedures. An exact numeral is provided for pupils' test results and these may be compared with test results of other learners in the same grade level. Yearly progress is reported based on test results for each pupil, with comparisons also made among schools, school districts and states (See Ediger, 2008).

Toward the other end of the continuum, experimentalism is emphasized with problem solving procedures as one approach. In an ongoing lesson or unit of study, pupils with teacher guidance identify a problem. The problem is clearly stated and based on pupil interests and purposes. Encouragement provides effort in pupil problem selection. Pupils need to do the learning and be active participants in the curriculum. The teacher serves as a resource person, helper and assistant (Dewey, 1916).

The learning process moves forward with pupils securing necessary information in problem solving with an hypothesis or tentative answer to the stated problem. Diverse reference sources are used such as concrete (excursions, objects, items, quality resource personnel, among others), semi-concrete (illustrations, video tapes, power point presentations, computer sources, among others) and abstract materials (basal textbooks, library books, magazines, newspaper articles, as well as other print materials). Pupils choose which reference sources provide needed information in answer to the problem. Learners engage with learning activities as they relate to individual differences, personal background information of participants, as well as those engaged in through scaffolding.

Information obtained require pupils to work collectively in problem solving and is a dynamic procedure. Respect for each other and for ideas obtained are musts. Ideas will need to be harmonized within a committee setting. Progress in problem solving comes from pupils accepting each other in a democratic setting.

Answers to the problem, from information secured, test the hypothesis. Learning is an active process and pupils with teacher guidance order their very own experiences in gathering subject matter as well as in testing an hypothesis. Pupils discover concepts and generalizations; they are not told answers to questions, but discover, through effort, needed content. Meaning and understanding occurs through interaction with others. Pupils interact with each other and with the teacher in problem solving situations. Sequence, ultimately, resides within the learner and not within the materials of instruction.

Problem solving also emphasizes one form of constructivism whereby the latter stresses the following:

- active involvement of learners in developing ongoing lessons and units of study.
- pupils working collaboratively in the curriculum.
- pupils interact with the teacher as in a dynamic social situation.
- evaluation stresses pupils working together with the teacher to improve learning situations.
- pupils guided to find their own answers to problems and questions.
- knowledge and skills are holistic and not factual, nor in isolated parts (See Everhart, 2009).

In addition to problem solving, there are additional approaches in stressing experimentalism whereby pupils have a large voice in ascertaining what to learn. William Heard Kilpatrick (1874-1965) emphasized a project method whereby pupils were wholeheartedly involved in also sequencing their own experiences. Here, pupils completed a project with an authentic procedure of constructing something concrete in nature (Ediger and Rao, 2003). The following general sequence may be followed by pupils with teacher assistance:

- pupil purposing. There needs to be a purpose in doing a project. These purposes come from the learner.
- pupil planning. Here, pupils collectively in a small group develop ordered, flexible steps for proceeding with the project.
- pupil executing or carrying out the plans to fruition.
- pupil judging the completed project in terms of desired criteria.

With Dr. Kilpatrick's project method, pupils are active learners, not passive recipients of knowledge. The teacher's role is to help, assist and guide, but not lecture. Pupil ownership of the curriculum is definitely in evidence. Within small groups of four to five pupils, there is peer interaction with support from the teacher. Quality interaction among committee members is salient as is the quality of the finished project.

Experimentalism is very much in vogue today with the following plans of instruction also being stressed by teachers:

- peer mediated instruction. Here, pupils work together on an activity with discussions ongoing until the task is completed. For example in reading, peers may agree upon a selection to be read and then, indepth, answer agreed upon questions and problems, collaboratively.
- pupil planning of a creative dramatics presentation from a history lesson/unit of study with agreed upon parts played by individuals in making history come live.
- reader's theater in which pupils individually practice reading aloud a play performance. Intonation of voice, pitch, accent, and juncture play important roles for each read aloud. The final presentation may be presented to other classrooms of pupils. There is considerable cooperation in planning such as who gets which play part and how the read aloud is to be given orally. Rehearsals are necessary for a good presentation.

In Summary

Two somewhat opposing schools of thought were presented in curriculum development. Behaviorism emphasizes precise objectives be established for pupil achievement. Either pupils do/do not attain these objectives as a result of teaching. Experimentalism, in contrast, stresses that objectives tend to arise as a lesson/unit of study progresses. Problem solving, as one example, emphasizes that pupils identify a problem and work collectively toward a solution. Pupils, here, with teacher guidance develop the curriculum with somewhat heavy pupil involvement.

REFERENCES

Dewey, John (1916), *Democracy and Education.* New York: The Macmillan Company.

Ediger, Marlow, and D. Bhaskara Rao (2002), *Psychology and Curriculum.* New Delhi, India: Discovery Publishing House.

.......................(2003), *Philosophy and the Curriculum.* New Delhi, India: Discovery Publishing House.

Ediger, Marlow (2008), "The American High School," *College Student Journal*, 42 (3), 814-817.

Everhart, Jerry (2009), "You Tube in the Classroom," *Science and Children*, 46 (9), 32-25.

Griffen, Sharon (2004), "Teaching Number Sense," *Educational Leadership*, 61 (5), 39-42.

Common Core Objectives versus Constructivism

Common core objectives are upon us and have been adopted by most of the states. These objectives and accompanying tests provide opportunities to make comparisons among all of the states in the union since all pupils on a grade level will be tested with the same test whereas the No Child Left Behind (NCLB) law of 2002 emphasized each state developing their own tests. This made for situations in which selected states had more complicated tests than did others and made comparisons between and among states impossible. Both the common core and NCLB stress the importance of teaching toward predetermined objectives whereas, in comparison, constructivism emphasizes input from pupils in ascertaining objectives of instruction. The question then arises as to who should determine objectives for learner attainment. Should objectives be determined on the federal, state, or local levels?

Additional Issues

Common Core as well as NCLB emphasizes the use of measurably stated objectives with its accompanying standardized tests. Generally multiple choice test items are taken by pupils, and these are machine scored so that a plethora of tests may be scored in a short time. Results are given in terms of percentiles, standard deviations and/or rank order. The school's test results are to be published in the local and state news media. Parents might then be informed of the progress made by their child's school or schools. There are problems in utilizing measurable stated objectives, as well as related tests, in teaching and learning situations, including the following:

- they tend to stress factual content, ideal for testing, since they are precise an leave little leeway for interpretation.
- they minimize higher levels of cognition such as critical and creative thinking as well as problem solving.
- they minimize the fine arts such as art and music which are difficult to measure precise progress therein with testing.
- they do not favor those who have a different style of preferred assessment than testing. Thus, in the visual and performing arts, performer observation techniques are utilized.
- they tend not to provide for individual differences within a test for a specific age level.
- they stress the saliency of "one size fits all."

It is indeed complicated to write high quality tests and have them pilot tested to take out vague test items, as well as test items possessing validity and reliability. When our middle aged child took a standardized writing test in junior high school, he came home at the end of the school day and said, "That was a test on grammar, not writing." This happened to be the case. Multiple choice test items were used therein, strictly. One can say the test was not valid in evaluating achievement in writing, but it may have possessed validity for measuring achievement in grammar, if it measured consistently.

Constructivism in the Curriculum

Constructivists tend to deemphasize testing pupils to notice achievement and progress. Rather, teacher observation is utilized as continuously as possible. Thus, within an ongoing lesson, if a pupil experiences difficulties, the teacher notices and may ask sequential questions until the learner determines the specific problem area and is then ready to continue. Thus, scaffolding as a method of instruction is being used; the teacher does not tell or say what the learner is to do to overcome the obstacle. Situations such as these assist the learner to ascertain on his/her own what to do sequentially with the teacher being a guide in instruction. Here, seat work is involved in this learning experience. Project methods harmonize well with constructivism as a psychology of learning. For example, a committee of four collaborate in constructing a model, directly related to the ongoing unit of study. With collaboration, the pupils decide upon the project which will assist in clarifying what is being learned. Thus, pupils feel that a purpose is involved in the construction activity. Sequentially, they plan how to do the project with the needed reference and art materials. Computer and other technological experiences are brought in as necessary. Thus, learners are able to move forward, following the planning of the project. They actually engage actively in doing and revising the plans as necessary. Working harmoniously is an objective of instruction in the project method and this includes developing criteria to ascertain the quality or lack thereof of the completed project.

Use can be made of the completed project by placing in a hallway display case for other pupils in school to observe. This project and others completed by pupils might well-bring on many vital learnings when observed by others. The writer has noticed, when supervising university student teachers in the public schools, how many pupils look at these displays of projects and discuss them with others. Inservice education is possible here, also, in that teachers of other classrooms have implemented ideas pertaining to the project method of instruction. Constructivists emphasize the following:

- minimize the use of tests to ascertain achievement. Rather, through teacher observation, the quality of pupil work is assessed and assistance given as needed which aids learners to move forward on their own.
- motivation for learning comes from within and the teacher must encourage and motivate pupils to achieve.

- negative situations in the classroom which hinder pupil progress need to be identified and omitted.
- stress the importance of learning activities which promote learner independence in ongoing activities.
- emphasize learner experiences which aid in pupils sequencing their own subject matter and skills.
- develop attitudes which encourage positive interactions in collaborative endeavors. Good human relations must be ongoing so that healthy attitudes are achieved in learning.
- teacher lecturing is frowned upon, rather the teacher is a guide and helper of pupil progress.

The Psychology of Learning

There are numerous comparisons to be made between common core and constructivism within the psychology of learning. Common core emphasizes teaching toward ends which are the predetermined objectives whereas constructivism stresses that objectives arise within a learning activity. The former emphasizes a curriculum determined within a framework by specialist while the latter focuses upon learner input in curricular experiences. Additional comparisons include the following:

- measurably stated objectives as compared to open ended experiences for learners.
- minimal pupil input versus encouragement of pupil involvement in ongoing activities.
- predetermined objectives in sequencing learnings as compared to objectives arising with an experience.
- testing to appraise pupil learning as contrasted with informal means of ascertaining achievement.
- a national curriculum versus locally developed units and lessons.

In conclusion

When the author began teaching in the public schools in the early 1950s, there were no mandated objectives by the sat or nation. He emphasized objectives which were of his own choosing. As a beginner teaching in a rural school, the following conclusions were drawn:

- pupils were learning, but was it at a satisfactory rate and was relevant content being emphasized? However, is there more certainty of what should be taught with the implementation of state and/or federally mandated objectives?
- the sequence of pupil learning was adjusted to what pupils were doing well in. It is indeed difficult to seamlessly sequence subject matter and skills as perceived by the learner, because diagnosis and remediation must still be stressed in teaching and learning situations. The teacher, presently, must still sequence learnings, however, these must be ordered to achieve NCLB or common core objectives. Constructivism is strong in advocating that sequence resides within the pupil in the public schools.
- teacher observation was used mainly to appraise pupil progress in an open-ended procedure. The curriculum then was very flexible as contrasted with NCLB as well as common core.
- the teacher sequenced learnings for pupils as well as raised questions to check comprehension of subject matter.
- a teacher determined and planned curriculum, generally, was in vogue.

Teachers were provided with the Reed Tracey Tests, at the beginning of the school year, to evaluate pupil achievement every six weeks in reading and arithmetic. The writer had a difficult time to harmonize his teaching with multiple choice items in the Tests. Thus, the thirteen pupils did not do well on the first Test. It was difficult to see that the test covered knowledge and skills in the basal readers. The thinking was a problem of validity. Who was right, the test writers or the teacher in ascertaining "what should be in the Test?" There was no one to report the test results to, including the county superintendent, which oversaw the rural schools. In teaching rural pupils, there was much of decentralization of public schools. The teacher or teachers had the position of principal, superintendent, guidance counselor and lunch room supervisor, among other tasks and responsibilities.

Presently, there is and has been much emphasis placed upon mandated standardized testing. Much faith is placed upon these tests, as providing exact and accurate information about learner progress. The writer does not have that much faith in testing, but agrees that well developed tests might well provide selected pertinent information, along with other data/evaluation sources. It appears that these tests appear too quickly on the horizon and possess the following problem areas:

- a lack of validity, in that do they truly measure what it is they are supposed to measure? Also, choosing what is relevant is difficult to ascertain, as in career and college readiness in the common core.
- reliability, being highly significant, is easier to determine as in test/retest, split half and alternate forms.
- factual content appears in multiple choice tests whereby it might be relatively easy to machine score, but are these important in many cases? For example, decision making is very significant for all individuals in a life like situation, but it cannot be measured in using paper/pencil testing situations. Making quality decisions is very salient in life's endeavors. Can a test determine pupil achievement better than an actual situation?

Mandated Testing of Pupils versus Constructivism

Mandated testing on selected grade levels for promotional purposes has proponents and opponents. Mandated testing provides data for use in tracking learner progress through the grades. It provides information on who graduates from high school. Mandated testing may provide information on how well pupils are achieving in school as well as pinpoint where sequential achievement has been lacking. A point of intervention is then emphasized to remedy or modify situations when a lull in progress appears.

Mandated testing has its negative side such as too many tests being administered in a given school year. Pupils might experience test anxiety and not do well in testing situations. Tests tend to evaluate pupils on factual information and not branch out to higher levels of cognition. They may not stress evaluating pupils on what is truly salient and difficult to measure. Mandates want precise data on pupils progress, not essay content whereby pupils have a greater voice in how to respond and organize ideas for writing.

Mandated testing then has advantages and disadvantages in indicating what pupils have learned.

Analyzing Mandated Testing

Mandated tests are given once a year to determine pupil promotion from one grade to the next. Measurement specialist state that high stakes testing such as this, should be determdined by more than a single test. There are too many variables affecting a pupil's achievement with a one shot approach. These variables include physical health, the involved mental status of the learner, as well as variations in the quality of atmosphere surrounding the time of test taking, among others. Second, teachers feel forced to spend hours of time drilling pupils for taking the test. Drill is definitely not perceived to be a recommended way of involving pupils in learning, according to educational psychologists. Third, selected academic or curricular areas get slighted if reading, arithmetic and science, only, are tested upon as in No Child Left Behind (NCLB) federal mandate. Balance in the curriculum emphasizes that social studies, art, music, and physical education, too, need to become a vital part of a well rounded set of experiences for pupils. Fourth, what is tested, gets taught. There are a plethora of news reports where this is true. School principals are under pressure to have pupils do well on tests for public relations endeavors. The results are published in local newspapers. No one desires to experience failure. Thus, teachers are coaxed to pressure pupils to achieve well on tests. Fifth, there are cases of dishonesty where pupils' answers have been changed or correct answers are given to pupils to up test scores, before they are sent to computers for scoring. Some have used the test directly in teaching, word for word as they appear on the mandated test. Sixth, a few educators say learning is cheapened when pupils are tested continuously on the content acquired. They indicate that learning should be its own reward. Seventh, selected reinforcement techniques such as giving prizes to pupils if they achieve well on tests may also be detrimental, according to some educators. Instead of learning for its own sake, pupils then work to achieve prizes for doing well. Eighth, little thought has been given in ascertaining how valid and reliable the test content actually is. Is the subject matter in mandated testing what pupils truly need to do well in school and in society? Ninth, teacher observation in terms of quality criteria is the best procedure to utilize in appraising pupils progress. Why? The teacher may almost immediately notice the kinds of assistance which need to be given learners as these observations are being made. Feedback from pupils within a specific learning situation provides teachers with information for ensuing objectives to emphasize in teaching and learning situations. These are ten salient reasons for not administering mandated tests to pupils (Ediger, 2008).

There are important reasons given for stressing mandated testing. Data from testing is used to track pupil achievement from one grade level to the next. Thus, teachers and school administrators may notice, on the monitor, sequential test scores of pupils and where progress was made as well as when a lack of progress occurred. Second, test scores communicate to parents how well their offspring is doing in school achievement. Objectivity is there with percentile ratings, for example, such as a child being on the fortieth percentile in mathematics. Parents, however, need to be informed as to the meaning of percentiles or other unit measures to ascertain pupil achievement such as stanines, or grade equivalents. Third objective measurements are used to convey information on learner progress. Instead of slogans on pupil achievement, there are precise measurements provided from test results. Thus, there is a "handle" on reporting learner achievement in numerical terms. Fourth, comparisons may be made between individuals and schools. Some believe then that to show realistic pupil progress, there need to be standards to indicate which schools are doing well and which need improvement, or even mandated changes in teachers and in school administrators for poor pupil performance. Fifth, forced changes need to be made in having teachers measure up and be held accountable. If pupils fail to achieve adequately, teachers are not performing well in teaching and learning. Thus, if a pupil is not promoted to the subsequent grade level due to a low test score, then this reflects upon the teacher. Other variables are left out of the equation such as poverty of the child. Sixth, parents should have the right for their offspring to attend a different school if test results show continuous failure of low performing schools. Thus, low performing schools can be identified through failure for their pupils to meet definite requirements. Seventh, the bully pulpit can be used by state and national officials to motivate pupil progress. Results from testing may always be criticized in terms of inadequate learner progress, regardless of improved achievement from the previous school year. Or, negative verbal statements made about what is deemed underperforming schools, the purpose being to "encourage" quality education. Eighth, financial rewards, in terms of merit pay, may be given to teachers of schools deemed to be high in achievement. It is relatively easy to look at test results as the indicator to ascertain which schools are doing well. Ninth, a nation losses out in world trade and prosperity if the educational system is not functioning well as measured by tests in making international comparisons. The school systems at the top in international comparisons will tend to do the best in economic competition. Tenth, pupils in schools who are close to making the mark for promotion may receive extra coaching since the average rate of doing well will be expanded in number, such as in adequate yearly progress (AYR). This may be detrimental to other pupils in the classroom (See Campbell, 2007).

Constructivism in Philosophy of Education

Constructivism as a philosophy of education stresses that pupils assist in setting standards for achievement in ongoing lessons and units of study. They develop knowledge and skills and it is up to the teacher to motivate intrinsically, encourage, and promote learner achievement. Thus, the teacher, as well as pupils, provide learning opportunities within ongoing units of study. Pupils are challenged, not forced to learn what is perceived to be important, as well as learner purposes are involved to pursue and achieve. Perceptions change as new experiences are encountered; knowledge and skills, too, are then modified. Knowledge and skills are tentative and subject to change, they are not measurable. Critical and creative thinking as well as problem solving are emphasized. The project method is also salient when pupils construct, make, and engage in hands on experiences in ongoing units of study.

Pupils then arrive at their own unique truths through experiences. Through interaction with others and with materials of instruction, the pupil experiences and develops his/her own conclusions. Responsibility for learning resides within the learner, not the teacher nor in textbooks. Teachers facilitate and help pupils to achieve the latter's goals; support for learning comes from teachers, but definitely not in lecture form. Consructivist teachers are able to steer away from a deductive stance of teaching to one of assisting pupils to perceive their own values in learning. A relaxed learning environment which supports pupil thinking and in developing subsequent activities emphasizes a facilitating teacher who guides pupil ownership of ongoing experiences. Pupils then construct their own experiences, knowledge and skills. They are active, not passive learners; learning by discovery is significant to constructivists' thinking in education. Motivation to learn depends upon the confidence of the involved pupil in acquiring what is useful and has purpose (See Mansilla and Gardner, 2008).

Vygotsky (1978) emphasized that pupils work in small groups so that ideas are shared and challenged; ideas then may "bounce off" the minds of individuals in a discussion setting. Learning occurs within a contextual authentic setting, not within a decontextualized lecture nor in testing situations. Assessment of learning is ongoing and continuous with teacher observation; assistance to learners is given as needed in helping pupils to experience what is necessary in learning.

Toward the other end of the continuum, with measurement philosophy of education, pupils reveal a definite amount of learning which can be shown in numerical terms. Either a pupil does/does not achieve an objective. There is no guesswork. E.L. Thorndike (1874-1949) expressed the heart of measurement philosophy. He stated that "Anything that exists, exists in some amount, and if it exists in some amount, it can be measured." The measurement movement then extended to all curriculum areas as well as in measuring attitudes and the affective domain. For example, in doing my doctoral dissertation in 1962-1963, I measured how student teachers affected pupil achievement in attitude development using the California Test of Personality. In this study, mathematics progress was measured using the mathematics section of the Iowa Test of Basic Skills. Thus, if anything exists, such as art, music and physical education achievement, these can be measured. Mathematics is as exact a science as any academic discipline and, no doubt, becomes the easist to measure to measure pupil growth and progress.

The measurement movement has certainly become strongly rooted in educational systems around the world as in the following:

- state and federal testing mandates
- a voluntary system to measure a random sample of pupils in achievement such as the National Assessment of Educational Progress (NAEP)
- data driven systems of instruction
- comparisons among nations from international test results.

A major weakness of measurement driven instruction is to ascertain in behavioral terms and prior to instruction what pupils are to learn. Is there that degree of certainty? Further problems in the selection of objectives, as well as in testing, include the following:

- might what is highly relevant be stated in precise measurable terms for pupil achievement, such as being a caring person as well as being a good citizen?
- factual knowledge of pupils is relatively easy to test; is too much emphasis then placed unon testing lower cognitive level objectives rather than critical and creative thinking, as well as problem solving?
- only what is measurable may be chosen as objectives for pupil attainment.
- may salient objectives be left out of the instructional arena when these are chosen prior to instruction?

- how much input should pupils have into curricular decisions within ongoing lessons and units of study such as in identifying a relevant problem area?

REFERENCES

Campbell, Peter (2007), "Edison is the Symptom, *NCLB* is the Disease," *Phi Delta Kappan*, 438-443.

Ediger, Marlow (2008), "Mental Health and the Curriculum," *Journal of Instructional Psychology*, 35 (1), 38-42.

Mansilla, Veronica Bolz and Howard Gardner (2008), "Disciplining the Mind," *Educational Leadership*, 65 (5), 14-19.

Vygotsky, Len (1978), *Mind in Society*. Cambridge, Massachusettes: Harvard University Press.

Chapter 5 Evaluation of Pupil Achievement

Teachers need to be aware of using different methods of pupil evaluation at appropriate intervals. There are salient concepts which teachers need to be cognizant of in the evaluation process. Each evaluation technique has a purpose in its use as well as when it is to be utilized. Thus, evaluation has significant reasons for individual usage. The purpose of this chapter will be to clarify meanings of each evaluation use.

Informal Evaluation Procedures

Somewhat continuously, the classroom teacher appraises pupils in ongoing activities throughout the school day. Teacher observation is then being utilized to notice what pupils have accomplished in a daily lesson plan as well as what should come subsequently in teaching and learning situations. The following activities provide points of intervention:

- when a word is not identified in reading
- when a pupil cannot think of a topic to write on
- when sequence in written work is lacking
- when the learner forgot what was to come next in an oral book report
- when a committee is not able to proceed in developing of an art project within a specific unit of instruction (See Cuban, 2008).

Each of the above is an example of assistance to be given when carefully observing pupil progress. Teacher observation is ongoing and feedback from learners provide information on how well pupils are achieving. The teacher may wish to take notes on the types of help which needs to be given and how effective the assistance was for each classmate.

Anecdotal statements, as another evaluation technique, are recorded and dated written comments pertaining to observed pupil progress. The content here comes from teacher observations made such as the following anecdotal statements:

- October 10. Alex volunteered too do an extra book report.
- October 14. Bill is anxious to respond to questions in class, but his answers are very limited due to hurrying.
- October 18. Maria has difficulties in thinking of ideas when writing poetry.
- October 22. Norma bothers others who want to complete an assignment (See Ray, 2006).

With written comments, the teacher may be able to observe a pattern of behavior for each child. Comments written must be accurate and concise. They should assist the teacher in making better curricular decisions to help learners achieve more optimally.

Studying lesson plans which were used in teaching might also be classified as an informal evaluation approach. Thus, a small group of three to four teachers may evaluate the lesson plan of a committee member to ascertain its quality in the instructional arena. If need be, the lesson plan may be modified and tried out with a set of learners to notice its effects to optimize achievement. The following might have been modified:

- the sequence of learning activities
- provisions made for individual differences among pupils
- constructivism incorporated to help in harmonizing styles of learning (Ediger, 2006).

Teacher written tests, too, may be considered as being an informal means to ascertain achievement. These need to be valid and reliable. Clarity of writing is of utmost importance. Vagueness in test item writing does not assist pupils in revealing in what they know. Test items should be developmental appropriate and on the understanding level of pupils. Multiple choice tests are frequently used here, There are rules for writing multiple choice test items such as:

- each response being plausible and of a similar length in order not to provide clues as to the correct answer.
- each response together with the stem making for a grammatically correct sentence.
- only one response being correct unless otherwise given in the test directions (Ediger, 2009).

True/false test items might also be written by the teacher. Guesswork is taken out of responding by having pupils indicate in writing what is incorrect in a test item.

Essay tests provide opportunities for pupils to construct their very own answers. Questions in an essay test need to be thought provoking and involve problem solving as well as be adequately delimited. The following then are two extremes to avoid in writing essay test items:

- What year was Jerusalem captured by the Crusaders? The answer requires a factual recall of a date and requires little in the line of thought and thinking.
- Write about the Crusades in world history. Volumes have been written on the Crusades and this topic is much too broad in scope for an essay test item (Ediger, 2008).

Adequately delimited test items might well be the following:

- Who were the Crusaders when they first organized in AD 1096 ?
- Why did people join the ranks in becoming a Crusader?

Essay tests reveal how well pupils write sentences which are grammatically correct as well as indicate spelling and handwriting skills. Evaluation should be based on correct information presented with the mechanical skills of writing graded separately. If pupils are ready and enough computers are available, they may use the word processor to construct answers. The latest in technology should be used in the curriculum. This, however, does not eliminate using longhand in written work. When supervising university student teachers in the public schools, several cooperating teachers stated they could not foresee the complete elimination of using paper and pen/pencil to communicate ideas. The writer advocates the use of word processors and the latest in technology whenever feasible, relevant and possible.

To objectify the evaluation process of essay responses, educators may recommend strongly that rubrics be used. Rubrics contain criterion to appraise essay responses. Generally, they are given on a five point scale. The criteria are then written out to serve as a guideline to appraise essay responses. The following is an example of a five point scale to use as a model to appraise responses from essay tests written in long hand:

- **Scale of five.** The essay contains accurate statements given in a clear, logical manner. The ideas are presented sequentially.
- **Scale of four.** The essay contains a few errors in information presented. But the information is presented in a logical and sequential manner.
- **Scale of three.** The essay contains errors in information; logic and sequence are lacking in selected situations.
- **Scale of two.** Errors in information distract from the essay as does logic in written sentences.
- **Scale one.** The essay needs rewriting after the weaknesses have been pinpointed.

Evaluation of Achievement of Pupil Achievement in Unit Teaching

Formative evaluation is emphasized during the time a unit of study is taught. Here, the teacher wishes to find out what pupils have learned and there still is time to make changes before the unit culminates. Formative evaluation then may occur at any point, prior to its ending. Purposes for formal evaluation include the following:

- to ascertain what needs reteaching
- to determine what has been mastered by pupils
- to add new salient objectives for pupil attainment
- to make decisions on necessary review of selected concepts and generalizations
- to appraise the general achievement level of involved learners
- to make needed modifications and changes in the curriculum (Ediger, 2009).

Formative evaluation stresses assessment along the way, instead of at the end of a unit of study only. Teacher written tests may be used, in part, in formative evaluation, such as multiple choice, true/false, essay, matching, and short answer tests. The teacher has a chance, in formative evaluation, to notice the effectiveness of his/her teaching. How successful was the teacher in the instructional arena involving unit teaching?

End of the unit appraisal pertains to *summative* evaluation. Here, the unit has been completed and the teacher desires to ascertain how much pupils have learned in achieving knowledge and skills objectives. Purposes inherent in summative evaluation are the following:

- have the instructional objectives been attained by pupils?
- what needs to be modified when teaching this unit the next time?
- are there other learning opportunities which might be more beneficial to learners than those used?
- should the order or sequence of activities be changed?
- did the evaluation techniques measure in a valid and reliable way?
- should a pretest be added so that progress may be measured using post-test minus pretest results? (See Beckstead, 2008).

Standardized Testing

With the measurement movement being in vogue, many standardized rests are purchased by states to notice mandated achievement. Standardized tests indicate that each pupil has the same test items for the grade level being tested, the directions for test administration are the same for all and the scoring key for computerized scoring is also the same. Generally, multiple choice test items are used since they may be scored with the same scoring key with exact, precise answers. Thus, on the print out, it is easy to notice the percentile rank of the pupil when compared to others having taken the same test. No allowances are made for language difficulties in speaking a different language than English. Nor are allowances made for slow learners, as well as those who are mentally retarded. Then, too, selected pupils need more time in test completion as compared to others. More variables result, if the teacher drills pupils on test taking procedures or uses a manual which assists pupils to secure higher test results.

There are further problems in that the test may not be valid for pupils if teachers have not had access to specific objectives directly related to items on the test, or if teachers did not carefully consider the objectives when teaching. The test may lack reliability if pilot studies were not run prior to standardization of the test. The Manual should provide specific results of validity and reliability. There are additional questions which arise pertaining to the use of standardized tests to measure pupil achievement:

- are the items relevant for pupils as citizens in society?
- does increasing test scores become the objective of schooling?
- do teachers and principals emphasize teaching to the test largely or only?
- does "what is on the test" count only or largely as teaching pupils?
- might the scope of the test be broadened to include such concepts as caring for others, having a positive attitude and being a good citizen?

- should the mandated test also include questions pertaining to measuring achievement in the social studies, art, music, and physical education, in order to stress *balance* in the curriculum? (See Wiggins and McTighe 2006).

Criterion Referenced Testing (CRT)

Whereas standardized testing stresses making comparisons among and between pupils' test results, CRTs emphasize the teacher teaching toward pupils achieving specific objectives of instruction. Comparisons in achievement then are not made among learners, but what is important is that all learners have ample opportunities to achieve the stated objectives. Some will take more time in doing so, as compared to others. There are no specific time limits here. The criterion in CRTs are the precisely stated objectives of instruction. Teachers need to realize the following in CRTS:

- it is clearly centered upon pupils achieving measurably stated objectives of instruction. Either, a pupil does/ does not attain an objective as a result of instruction. For some advocates of CRTs, the objectives may be more open ended. In CRTs, a variety of learning opportunities may be implemented with the following standards in evidence:
    * a variety of experiences to achieve objectives may be used here.
    * proper sequence in choosing and implementing learning opportunities is salient.
    * teacher feedback received of learner achievement due to the success or lack thereof in goal attainment.
    * clarity in objectives so that the teacher knows if ordered objectives have been attained (See Gill, 2008).

Benchmarks may be set up along the way as goals for pupils to attain by a selected time. The purposes here are to stay on track and have a specific time set to achieve a definite point on the continuum of learners progress. The question to be raised, "Are pupils making adequate progress in goal attainment?" Should pupils then have achieved more than where they are at the present time? The established benchmark will attempt to answer that question.

Conclusion

There are a plethora of beliefs pertaining to how pupil achievement should be evaluated. Teachers and school administrators must be well versed in each procedure in order to make quality decisions in curriculum improvement. Individual differences need to be provided for so each pupil may attain as optimally as possible.

REFERENCES

Beckstead, Larissa (2008), "Scientific Journals: A Creative Assessment Tool", *Science and Children*, 46 (3), 22-26.

Cuban, Larry (2008), "The Perennial Reform: Fixing School Time", Phi Delta Kappan, 90 (4), 241-250.

Ediger, Marlow (2006), "Writing in the Mathematics Curriculum", *Journal of Instructional Psychology*, 33 (2), 120-123.

Ediger, Marlow 2008), "The American High School", *College Student Journal,* 42(3), 814-817.

Ediger, Marlow (2009), "Reading Comprehension in the Science Curriculum", *Reading Improvement*, 46 (2), 78-80.

Ediger, Marlow (2009), "Scope in the Social Studies," *Edutracks*, 8 (6), 14-16.

Gill, Sharon Ruth (2008), "The Comprehension Matrix: A Tool for Designing Comprehension Instruction", *The Reading Teacher*, 63 (2), 106-113.

Ray, Katie Wood (2006), "What Are You Thinking?", *Educational Leadership*, 64(2), 58-62.

Wiggins, Grant and Jay Me Tighe (2006), "Examining the Teaching Life", *Educational Leadership*, 63 (6), 26-30.

Chapter 6 Psychology of Testing and Evaluation

Much emphasis is being placed upon testing as a means of determining what pupils have learned in school. *Behaviorism* is emphasized here with its measurement philosophy of determining what pupils have acquired. State mandated tests are used to ascertain what pupils have learned and achieved when comparing one state with another in the union. These test results may also be utilized in contrasting school districts in pupils making progress, or lack thereof, from one school year to the next. The National Assessment of Educational Progress (NAEP) is given to a representative set of students in the United States each year in comparing cohorts from one school year to the next. Then too, there are international comparisons among nations such as the Third International Mathematics and Science Study (TIMSS). Behaviorism, as a psychology of learning is being stressed with its measurable results given in numerical terms.

Toward the other side of the equation is *constructivism* which does not depend upon test results to ascertain pupil achievement. Constructivism emphasizes pupils learning by discovery which does not permit testing at each specific, flexible step of learning. In fact, tests are unimportant. Teacher observation can be a major approach in evaluating progress and achievement (Ediger and Rao, 2003).

Behaviorism and Measurement

Since the early 1900s, behaviorists have had a strong backing in measuring pupils in different areas of achievement.

E. L. Thorndike (1874-1949) and associates developed standardized tests to measure curricular achievement in arithmetic, spelling, and reading, among others. Arithmetic is an accurate science in that there are exact answers in addition, subtraction, multi-plication, and division, among other operations on number. Behaviorism can work well in these situations with the use of multiple choice test items where there is only one right answer of four plausible distractors to choose from. In the spelling of English words, there usually is a correct way of spelling a word. However, there are exceptions: catalog, catalogue.

Presently, there are many areas in which measurement philosophy is used including personality tests, vocational aptitude and interest tests, power tests, analogy tests, tests which predict success in a given endeavor, among a plethora of others. Testing has become a major enterprise with companies and corporations making hugh profits from developing and selling tests (See Brady, 2008).

Validity is a very important concept in testing. A test then needs to measure what it purports to measure. It does take much money and time to develop any test such as one, for example, which claims to measure readiness for reading. There are problems in determining validity, such as in the area of teaching social studies. Names, dates and places lend themselves well for test items in history as do many facts. The following are not that concise to measure in the social studies:

- evaluating qualities of good citizenship
- respecting others as well as caring for others
- good human relations
- self realization and its component parts (Ediger, 2008).

Attempts, of course, have been made to measure these more abstract and general concepts.

In addition to validity, reliability is a second major concept to stress in measurement, whereby a test measures consistently for any trait such, as readiness for reading. To determine reliability, the following procedures are used test/retest, alternate forms, split half, and/or a combination of these approaches. In using personality tests, the following can vary much, for example, in test/retest situations:

- how pupils feel toward school as well as toward the teacher, from one testing to the next
- how pupils react to each academic discipline in time.

The feeling dimension may vary considerably from one time to the next. Fatigue, an unhappy experience, and unfavouable testing environment enter into the equation. The writer when taking a standardized test at a university experienced a crowded room with no air conditioning at that time. The worst part was an adjacent student chewing gum loudly! Cognitive learnings are more stable as compared to the affective dimension, but even then forgetting occurs or learnings become hazy (Ediger, 2009).

Behaviorism, also includes master learning in that pupils achieve predetermined objectives. These objectives, developed prior to instruction, are the targets the teacher aims toward when choosing learning activities for pupils. Testing and measuring will ascertain if these objectives have been attained. The assumption is that once the test results indicate objectives have been achieved, then learning has occurred in the desired direction. There are several problems here:

- how stable are these learnings and does forgetting soon occur?
- how relevant are the objectives in terms of future use for learners? They appear to be absolutes and written in stone.
- how might pupils be involved in the curriculum? Behaviorism permits little leeway here (See Ahmad 2009).

Evaluation through Observation

What might evaluation look like without tests? The writer got a new set of eye glasses from an optometrist for $385. He could not read with these glasses; they were not appropriate for reading which is truly a highly prized skill possessed. He returned to the optometrist for a recheck of what was needed in terms of eye glasses. The optometrist ran through the procedure again with his machine and stated the prescription was correct and I should be able to read well with these eye glasses. The trouble was my vision with the glasses was very poor. I was unable to secure new needed frames for the old glasses. By chance a week later, I picked up my wife's eye glasses to see how the print looked. To my amazement, her glasses from Walgreens, costing $22 was a perfect match for reading. I did my own matching of eye glasses from those on the store's counter and came home with somewhat perfect glasses with no accompanying headaches from reading.

Comparing my experiences with eye glasses and standardized tests for pupils in the school setting, I have pondered much over the following:

* are there better approaches in determining pupil achievement as compared to traditional testing? The optometrist mentioned above was not able to determine correct reading glasses by using the latest in technology.
* should pupils show more of their sequential learnings directly such as in discussions in all curriculum areas, reading aloud, use of arithmetic from daily assignments and from functional use of number, doing science experiments, engaging in the complete act of thought in problem solving, written work in each subject matter field, higher levels of cognition (critical and creative thinking, drawing inferences, cause/effect, as well as comparison/contrast).
* should diversity in evaluation be shown with pupils making drawings, diagrams, charts, and graphs to reveal what has been learned? (See Teale and Campbell, 2007).

The above listed asterisked items indicate that multiple choice test items would not be used, but teacher observation might well take its place. However, the accountability movement wants data, generally standardized test results, to show pupil progress in time. There are a plethora of questions which may be raised about multiple choice test items:

- are they truly objective since human beings write test items?
- do they bias test taking/evaluation in that one kind of assessment technique is being used?
- how can test writers be certain that what is written is practical and relevant?
- with sometimes large standards of error of measurement within a test, how accurate is it to rank and compare pupils in test results
- what might the correlation be between test scores and future success at the work place and in society of an individual?
- how salient is it to include affective learnings in test taking? Attitudinal goals are equally important as compared to cognitive objectives, according to many educators.
- is measurable content picked for inclusion, such as facts, to the detriment of salient objectives such as caring and empathetic human beings?

Constructivism, as a psychology of learning, is quite different as compared to behaviorism. Instead of predetermined objectives for pupil attainment, consructivists emphasize that pupils are actively involved in learning whereby there is dynamic interaction among the teacher, the learning activity, and other pupils. Pupil learning by discovery is stressed rather than the teacher lecturing/explaining to pupils. The teacher's role is to stimulate learner thinking in ongoing experiences in the curriculum. The purposes of the pupil are salient to foster; they have individual reasons for perceiving a need to achieve vital personal goals. Instead of answering a pupil's question directly in an ongoing lesson/unit of study, The teacher raises a related question to assist learners to think and come up with a relevant answer. The interests of pupils then are important considerations in the learning process. These interests propel learning and help pupils to put forth much effort in the classroom. Problem solving experiences is a good example in that a problem comes from learners. Learners develop a tentative answer or hypothesis to the problem. The hypothesis is tested in an authentic learning situation resulting in its acceptance, modification, or rejection. Problems are:

- identified by pupils with teacher assistance and clarification.
- refined so they may be tested with the use of relevant experiences and activities.
- new problems, identified by pupils, might well arise in these situations.
- information sources to solve problems are used. The teacher always assists, encourages, and helps pupils in inquiry learning (Dewey, 1916).

How does the teacher assist in sequential pupil learning? A few examples might well indicate teacher involvement:

- instead of lecturing, explaining, and telling, the teacher asks ordered questions, leading the pupil to an answer.
- when pupils are reading to secure information, they may have problems with word recognition. Here, the teacher assists with the pupil using context clues, sounding out the word if phonetically spelled, looking for smaller words within the larger word, and/or dividing it into syllables.

REFERENCES

Ahmad, Sajjad (2009), "Evolving a Framework for Teaching and Learning," *Edutracks*, 8 (9),11-12.

Brady, Marion (2008), "Cover the Material or Teach Students to Think," *Educational Leadership*, 65 (5), 64-67.

Dewey, John (1916), *Democracy and Education*. Mew York: The Macmillan Company.

Ediger, Marlow (2008), "The Old Order Amish and the Social Studies," *Viewpoints*, 38 (4), 13-16.

Ediger, Marlow (2009), "The Principal in the Teaching and Learning Process," *Education*, 129 (4), 574-578.

Ediger, Marlow, and D. Bhaskara Rao (2003), *Psychology and Curriculum.* New Delhi, India: Discovery Publishing House.

Teale, William H., and Linda B. Gambrell (2007), "Raising Urban Student's Literacy Achievement by Engaging in Authentic, Challenging Work," *The Reading Teacher*, 60 (8), 728-739.

Teaching and Learning is more than Setting Standards

The setting of standards for pupils to achieve has become a national past time in education. State standards and national standards have become salient topics for writing as well as for speaking at national education conferences. It almost appears that the only important concept pertaining to teaching is standards. The standards movement has its initial beginnings in behaviorism as a psychology of learning. E. L. Thorndike (1874-1946) advocated that "whatever exists, exists in some amount, and if it exists in some amount, it can be measured." Tests were then developed as time went on in mathematics, reading, science, social studies and spelling, among others, to measure achievement in these academic/ curriculum areas.

Generally, multiple choice test items are written by selected educators and policy-makers to measure achievement. Test results then can be evaluated rather quickly with printouts, from computers, which tell how well a pupil, school, and/or school system is performing numerically. Precision is involved such as a pupil ranking on the fiftieth percentile, for example, meaning that for every 100 pupils tested, fifty are above and fifty below the fiftieth percentile. With machine scoring, mass numbers of tests may be scored in a relatively short period of time.

Standardization of Tests

Measurement of pupil achievement has usually gone in the

direction of standardized test use. Standardized tests emphasize the following:

- the directions for test taking are clearly written and are the same for all pupils taking the test.
- the time limits for test taking are the same for all.
- the scoring key is the same for all pupils taking the test on a particular grade level.
- raw scores of pupils from test taking then are compared with those of the norm group in the Manual. This provides percentiles, stanines, grade equivalent, and/ or age equivalent ranks. Percentiles are generally used and tend to be the easiest to understand.

Orderliness and specificity are key concepts in measurement philosophy of evaluation. Standardized test results emphasize comparing one pupil with another and one school/ school system with another. Comparisons in achievement might well also involve comparisons among states and nations.

Goals in making these comparisons are numerous such as:

- eliminating achievement gaps between and among different minority/majority groups of pupils.
- providing a standard for grade promotion.
- identifying weak schools and working toward a "turn around".
- permitting pupils to attend satisfactory schools which have met appropriate standards.
- free tutoring given to failing pupils.
- topping the list among nations of the world in academic achievement with international tests.

There are a plethora of criticisms in using measurement philosophy in determining achievement of pupils which includes the following:

- only what can be measured in achievement become test items on tests. Thus, factual test items accrue. This leaves out many important facets of accomplishment such as being a good citizen, having empathy toward others and treating others with respect. Attempts made in testing on the last three concepts have made for low reliability in test results.

- omission of selected curriculum areas in testing due to a focus on the basics of reading and mathematics. Science may be added also, but social studies, the fine arts, and physical education are omitted as in No Child Left Behind (NCLB).
- unreasonable standards to achieve for English Language Learners (ELL), special needs learners, and slow learners. These pupils must meet the same standards as do other levels of pupil achievement such as the gifted and the talented.
- time limits for test taking being the same for all. There are pupils who need more time to answer questions on tests as compared to others due to individual differences.
- multiple choice test items used in testing. Factual knowledge is easiest to test upon. These limit pupils in evaluating thinking abilities. Critical thinking and problem solving are very salient in school and in society.
- omission of any reference to determining achievement in *discussions.* In school and in society, much emphasis is placed upon discussions to assist in analyzing and synthesizing ideas.
- high stakes testing involved. With high stakes testing, one test determines promotion of pupils to the next grade level in NCLB. This is an inadequate system of evaluation. More sources of information should be used here in addition to high stakes test scores. There are too many reasons why a test score was low for a pupil on the day of testing such as ill health, tenseness about home ituations, and emotional upsets.

Further questions and problems arise when viewing test items themselves. Too frequently, people feel that a test score is an absolute. However, tests are developed by human beings and they attempt to measure what is felt to be salient. There are problems in writing test items such as are they truly valid? Not all schools will have stressed the same objectives and thus there are learners who have not experienced that which is covered in a standardized test. Test items, too, in selected cases may not have been written with clarity, even if upmost care is taken in their writing. Computer glitches have caused heart ache for selected parents who received noticed their offspring had failed only to find out later that a glitch in scoring was involved. Mass numbers of tests are scored each school year with the accountability movement in vogue.

Teachers have drilled students on test taking before a standardize test is given such as the NCLB. Drill amounts to memorization and educational psychologists frown upon drill as a major method of teaching. It is more important for pupils to understand and attach meaning to what is taught. Learners, also, need to perceive purpose in learning. It would be difficult for a pupil to perceive purpose in endless amount of drill, merely to do well on a test. Testing is not an authentic task; people in society do not show their talents and abilities through testing, but by actually performing work in a life like situation. Certainly, a correlational study should be made of how test scores on standardized tests relate to success at the work place. Do tests truly measure what is salient to know and do in order to succeed in society?

Adequate yearly progress (AYP) has been almost impossible to achieve in No Child Left Behind. Schools are almost destined to fail with AYP goals to be met by 2014.

Generally, Manuals are developed to assist pupils in studying for taking a standardized test. It would be important to know if there is a level playing field in that all have access to the same/similar kind of tutoring, prior to test taking. What about including family income levels, nutrition, safety, and a rich home/community learning environment? The profit motive is involved in developing tests and accompanying Manuals. The profit motive should not over take attempts to ascertain how well pupils are truly achieving (Ediger 2001).

Constructivism in Teaching

Constructivism as a psychology/philosophy of instruction does not place major emphasis upon stating objectives prior to instruction. However, there are general guidelines in which direction instruction will be taking place. Instead of determining objectives, prior to instruction, the teacher guides learners to attach meaning to and sequence learning experiences. It is the learner who will sequence or order experiences; the teacher encourages and assists pupils in achievement. The focal point of instruction is upon the pupil. Each pupil possesses unique differences from others. The teacher needs to understand the background of each learner in order to understand previous experiences of pupils. Responsibility for learning resides within each pupil. Motivation for learning differs from child to child, and the teacher needs to properly motivate pupils in the classroom. If a pupil does not understand a concept or generalization, the teacher raises questions for which the learner thinks about answers, which in sequence lead to understanding and meaning. He/she does not lecture ready made knowledge and skills for pupil digestion, but rather helps learners to find their own information.

Problem solving emphasizes constructivism in teaching and learning. Here, pupils in an authentic setting identify a relevant problem for which solutions need to be sought. The problem possesses relevance and requires diligence as well as effort in working toward a solution. An hypothesis is developed and tested with vital information gathered from a variety of sources. The hypothesis is then accepted, modified, or rejected. New problems may arise in the ongoing experience for which solutions are needed.

Project methods also stress elements of constructivism in that a concrete product is ultimately produced. Thus, a purpose for the project is envisioned by learners. The purpose, for example, is to develop a model or object, directly arising from interests developed within the unit of study being pursued. Specific plans are made for the construction activity which are then carried out and results in the final product. Evaluation standards need to be Crafted to appraise the product.

Committee endeavors are involved in doing projects as well as for problem solving. Cooperatively developed standards for each experience is salient. In each activity, pupils are heavily involved in sequencing their very own learnings. Interest in the experience provides effort and motivation for learning. Pupils are actively involved in ongoing learning experiences and this is an ideal emphasized by constructivists.

There is considerable interaction among pupils in committee endeavors, based on their interests. Pupils are heavily involved in ordering and perceiving sequence in tasks pursued. They assist in determining objectives, learning activities, integrating subject matter, as well as appraising achievement. The teacher has important responsibilities in being a guide, a helper and one who is able to motivate and encourage learners in ongoing experiences. Pupils generate knowledge and skills from past and ongoing experiences. Teachers do not impart knowledge and skills, but rather assist pupils to make discoveries inductively.

In Summary

Two somewhat opposing schools of thought were emphasized in teaching and learning situations. Measurement theory stresses the use of testing to evaluate achievement pupil achievement. Here, multiple choice test items are used to ascertain learner progress in learning. Data from test results are highly precise and presented in numerical terms. The objectives for the test are predetermined and available for teachers as guidelines to use in teaching. Specific levels of accomplishment for each learner need to be met in order to be promoted to the next grade level or to exit from high school. Teaching toward pupils achieving precise objectives is salient.

Toward the other end of the continuum, constructivism is quite open ended and leaves pupil leeway in the selection of objectives, learning opportunities and evaluation procedures. The teacher is a guide and motivator of pupil achievement. Learning by discovery is a key component in instruction.

REFERENCE

Ediger, Marlow and D. Bhaskara Rao (2002), *Psychology and Curriculum*. New Delhi, India: Discovery Publishing House.

Cooperative Learning and the Pupil

Much writing in professional journals and speeches presented at teacher education conventions pertain to the importance of cooperative learning. Pupils are to share ideas as well as engage in small group work, rather than in individual endeavors. This philosophy of instruction is, in part, based on the writings of Vygotsky (1933-1978). Vygotsky believed that pupils learn best in social situations whereby ideas circulate among members in the group. As these ideas "bump off the minds" of participants, they are learned by members.

Learning in social situations may be compared with individual endeavors whereby each pupil works on assignments, tasks, and problem solving experiences by the self. To be sure, learning opportunities will not be cooperative nor individualistic continuously, but the emphasis will be on one as compared to the other, during a given school day (Ediger, 2007).

Advantages of Cooperative Learning

There are a plethora of reasons which may be given in emphasizing cooperative learning. The following, among others, are salient:

- decisions made in organizations, clubs and councils, are made with within a membership. The larger unit may be quite formal with its strict hierarchical lines of organization or flexible when the informal group is quite small and there is less need for formality. Group interaction among its members include the following:

* pupils, as well as adults, interact frequently in group settings. This may be true of informal conversations among participants.
* individuals might well ask for assistance from a group when problems arise and help is necessary.
* feelings of security may be found in a small group setting.
* pupils like to feel they belong in a group.
* individuals are social beings and like to affiliate with others (See Maslow 1954).

Problem solving methods tend to stress small group endeavors in the classroom setting. Here, pupils with teacher assistance identify a problem area in an ongoing unit of study. The problem involves deliberation and thinking is stressed. Thus in a social studies unit of study, pupils may identify the following:

- Why did the Ottoman Empire collapse at the end of World War I?
- Why did Great Britain receive mandates to rule Palestine, Iraq and Jordan whereas France mandated Syria and Lebanon following World War I?
- What was the significance of the Balfour Declaration of 1917 as well as the MacMahon/Hussein correspondence of 1915?
- How did each of the Mandates affect the Middle East? (Ediger, 1997).

Problems chosen need to be developmentally appropriate. Four to five classmates should be on each committee of their very own choosing. Reference materials need to be discussed and readily available. Encyclopedia, library books, resource personnel who have lived in the Middle East, video tapes, and especially the computer and the internet are valuable sources of information in gathering information to assist in solving the above asterisked problems.

The teacher needs to be certain that pupils understand flexible rules for engaging in committee work; these include the following:

- each member needs to participate
- no one should dominate committee procedures
- participants need to communicate ideas clearly
- questions should be asked if a contribution is not understood or if a new problem arises
- courtesy toward and consideration for others are two concepts to emphasize in small group endeavors
- the teacher is a consultant, not a lecturer nor bystander
- the committee is to work for the good of the group (see Parker, 2001).

If more than one committee is in operation, then progress reports may be made to other committees. An atmosphere of encouragement to do good work must prevail. Summaries of committee endeavors may also be made to the total class. These can be made in chart form and posted on a nearby wall. If a project is involved, the completed construction item, too, needs to be displayed so that classmates and pupils from other classrooms may observe and ask questions about each. The completed work might well be assessed in terms of the following criteria:

- accuracy stressed in the total activity.
- active participation by each committee member.
- neatness in ongoing experiences.
- appreciation for committee work.
- positive attitudes toward others (Ediger, 2008).

Problem solving and project methods might well lend themselves to additional cooperative activities in ensuing lessons and units of study. Pupil interests and purposes should be inherent in each identified problem and project. It is the pupil that needs to do the learning and the teacher needs to supervise the ongoing experiences and informally evaluate progress to determine if learners achieved objectives of instruction.

It is important that each member participates fully in cooperative learning. The writer's daughter did not appreciate cooperative learning as a junior high school student when working as a member of the yearbook committee. She felt alone in doing most of the work while the other members were content to be observers. The teacher must observe that all participate in completing an activity. Members work together to fulfil plans in problem solving or in completing a project (See Bembemutty, 2008).

Pupils Individually Achieving Objectives

Somewhat opposite in grouping pupils for instruction is to assist learners to work individually on an activity. There are educators who state that individual preferences versus cooperative learning pertain to learning styles and not that one is superior to the other. Perhaps, both are salient in that life itself emphasizes interaction with others as well as being able to do things by the self. Sometimes, the two are inseparable. There are a plethora of experiences which are highly profitable for individual endeavors. These include the following:

- reading activities in ongoing units of study or for sheer enjoyment.
- writing experiences in different curriculum areas as in narrative, expository, and creative endeavors.
- viewing and listening to content from a video tape.
- practising an oral report to be given in class.
- doing a drawing to summarize acquired learnings from a reading/ listening activity.
- inventing and playing a game (See Noddings, 2008).

With individual work, the pupil needs adequate background information to participate in achieving an objective. He/she must monitor the self to notice if progress is being made. Self-reflection is salient in reviewing what has been learned, what is left to learn and additional learnings desired. It is significant for the learner to become efficacious, thus becoming increasingly confident with ample needed knowledge, skills, and appropriate attitudes. Many of these behaviours are equally salient in cooperative learning.

With individual tasks, the teacher may carefully monitor leaner progress, for example, in specific learnings such as the following:

* answering questions from a basal textbook covering subject matter read.
* doing a bulletin board display.
* pantomiming a scene from a library book.
* writing specific kinds of poetry in an English assignment.
* drawing a map showing historic location of a place.
* completing a mathematics assignment involving addition of fractions.
* setting up a science experiment (See Sharma and Sharma, 2009).

There are a plethora of individual learning experiences for pupils. Each of the above asterisked activities might also be done in a cooperative setting. The point is that pupils should achieve as optimally as possible, be it in individual or in cooperative endeavors.

Criteria to utilize in evaluating pupils on individual tasks performed include the following:

- perceived effort put forth in learning.
- quality of meticulous work in ongoing experiences.
- revealing an attitude of desiring to do well in assignments as well as in voluntary endeavors.
- use of leisure time in a profitable way.
- self-evaluation of ongoing as well as of completed school work.
- reflection of what has been learned and identification of what is left to learn.
- a desire to learn in school and in society (See Phillips, *et al.*, 2008).

Balance in the Curriculum

The teacher needs to seek balance between cooperative learning and individual endeavors. Both procedures are highly worthwhile if they:

- assist in providing for optimal learner progress.
- engage pupils in learning.
- secure and maintain learner interests.
- help pupils to feel that achieving stated objectives is indeed worthwhile.
- guide pupils to perceive sequence in learning.
- provide for learning styles of pupils.
- emphasize relevance in the curriculum (Ediger, 2009).

In closing

A variety of learning opportunities must be used to promote individual and social development of pupils. In addition to those alluded to previously, ample experiences need to be provided in the use of technology and computers in the achievement of objectives of instruction. Thus, pupils might well work on programs individually as well as in cooperative learning. Computerized programs need to be stimulating, challenging, and developmentally appropriate.

REFERENCES

Bembemutty, Heifer (2009), "Feeling-of-Knowing Judgment and Self-Regulation of Learning," *Education*, 129 (4), 589-598, Discovery Publishing House Ltd.

Ediger, Marlow (1997), *The Holy Land*. Kirksville, Missouri: Simpson Publishing Company, Discovery Publishing House Ltd.

Ediger, Marlow (2008), "Psychology of Parental Involvement in Reading," *Reading Improvement*, 45 (1), 46-52, Discovery Publishing House Ltd.

Ediger, Marlow (2009), "Technical Education, the Work Place and the Student," *ATEA Journal*, 36 (2), 18-19, Discovery Publishing House Ltd.

Ediger, Marlow and D. Bhaskara Rao (2007), *Language Arts Education*. New Delhi, India: Discovery Publishing House Ltd., Discovery Publishing House Ltd.

Maslow, Abraham (1954), *Motivation and Personality*. New York: Harper and Row, Discovery Publishing House Ltd.

Noddings, Nel (2008), "All Our Students Thinking," *Educational Leadership,* 65 (5), 9-13, Discovery Publishing House Ltd.

Parker, Walter C. (2001), *Social Studies in Elementary Education*. Columbus, Ohio: Prentice-Hall, Inc., Chapter Eleven, Discovery Publishing House Ltd.

Phillips, Antionette S., *et al.*, 2008), "Enhancing A Curriculum: A Focus on the Developmental Process," *College Student Journal*, 42 (4), 1070-1 074, Discovery Publishing House Ltd.

Sharma, Mala, and Sumar Sharma (2009), "Attitude of Science Teachers Towards the Project Method," *Edutracks*, 8 (6), 40-43. Printed in India, Discovery Publishing House Ltd.

Vygotsky, Lin (1933-1978), *Mind in Society*. Cambridge, Massachusetts: Harvard University Press, Discovery Publishing House Ltd.

Chapter 9 Pointers in Teaching the Language Arts

There are selected pointers in teaching the language arts which include listening, speaking, reading, an writing. Thus, the teacher has these in mind as teaching and learning accrue. Each pupil then receives needed attention to attain as optimally as possible. Learning activities must be chosen on the basis of reflecting the ensuing relevant pointers.

Language Arts Instruction

The language arts teacher needs to observe that all pupils in class are actively involved in achieving. Pupils' attention may also be drawn to the learning experience through appropriate teacher voice inflection (stress, pitch, and enunciation), and/or using instructional examples which challenge and draw the interests of the learner. Interest is a powerful factor in learning and might well draw attention to the ongoing activity. Scaffolding is an important technique to use in the instructional arena in assisting learners to attain more optimally. Also, the kind of activity may need changing to prevent boredom; a flexible language arts teacher possesses a repertoire of diverse kinds of activities which meet individual pupil needs in achieving objectives of instruction (Ediger and Rao, 2009).

Second, purpose needs to be involved in ongoing activities. Thus, if pupils understand reasons for active participation in sequential experiences, they will attend more efficiently in teaching and learning situations. For example, if pupils are to write a friendly letter, the contents may be sent snail mail or e-mail to the intended person. The *purpose* here is to communicate ideas and happenings to a friend. Technology, such as the word processor, should be utilized when it assists learners in achievement and communicating effectively. Technology and its use is the wave of the future and its use will be increasingly inherent in all of school and in society. Purpose then may include the written subject matter as well as the many uses of technological procedures.

Third, meaning is a salient concept to stress in the language arts. With meaning, the pupil makes sense of and in ongoing activities. Experiences then mean something to the pupil as well as possessing relevancy. If a pupil does not attach meaning to the language arts activity, he/she will misunderstand how to write individual parts of the friendly letter as well as be unable to think of vital ideas to communicate (Ediger, 2007).

Fourth, grammar and usage should be taught as needed in writing and speaking. The kinds and types of errors made provide a checklist for helping pupils individually as necessary. For instance, if a pupil does not use modifiers at the appropriate place, assistance is provided at this point in time. The fact of the matter is to emphasize and remedy pupil needs, such as agreement of subject and predicate at the proper time of intervention in written work. When supervising university student teachers in the public schools, the writer noticed lessons taught on grammar completely divorced from practical and utilitarian concerns in writing. It appeared that pupils were not motivated to learn as well as not applying that which was being stressed. Learners must feel the importance of subject matter to be acquired (See also Wagstaff, 1994).

Fifth, virtual education needs incorporation for those who benefit from this technological approach. Online education might well be one salient method of learning. Thus, pupils may progress on their own in home and in school. Scheduling is left up to the learner when the opportunity presents itself. Here, the learner can proceed at his/her own pace. For high school students, in particular, the chances to blend brick and mortar education with online course work should make for a flexible schedule to meet personal needs in instruction. When readiness permits, each pupil may benefit from online education. Recovery credit is also possible for previously unfinished course work in a specific facet of the secondary language arts curriculum. Intrinsic motivation might well make it possible to pursue higher or technical education at a sooner time than otherwise would be possible. Technology must be utilized to achieve objectives of instruction in a meaningful way for all learners (See August, *et al.,* 2005).

Sixth, a quality program of assessing pupil progress should be in the offing with valid and reliable testing, be they multiple choice or essay test items. If validity and reliability are lacking, testing may not possess much significance. Teachers receive feedback from the tests in terms of meeting learner needs. Selected content may then need reteaching, review, as well as indepth teaching. Machine scored multiple choice test items provide results to the teacher in analyzing responses and then noticing errors common to all pupils taking the test. Well developed rubrics should be used to score essay test results. Again, from the evaluation, teachers take careful notice of what needs added attention in teaching and learning situations.

Seventh, to develop self efficacy, the language arts instructor must grow in knowledge and skills by taking graduate courses on a university campus or through online course work; attending state and national conventions pertain to improving instruction in reading, writing, speaking, and listening including the National Council Teachers of English (NOTE), the International Reading Association (IRA) conventions; as well as reading subject matter from journals and from content in teacher education textbooks.

REFERENCES

August, D., *et al.,* (2005), "The Critical Role of Vocabulary Development for English Language Learners," *Learning Disabilities Research and Practice*, 20 (1), 50-57.

Ediger, Marlow (2007), "Meaning in Reading Instruction," Reading Improvement, 41 (4), 217-221.

Ediger, Marlow, and D. Bhaskara Rao (2009), *Reading Curriculum and Instruction*. New Delhi, India: Discovery Publishing House Ltd.

Wagstaff, J. (1994), *Phonics That Work*, New York: Scholastic.

Chapter 10 Plans of Reading Instruction

There are a plethora of plans available to assist teachers in the teaching of reading. Each plan has strengths and will be discussed briefly. The reading teacher needs to study and appraise each plan with the intent of incorporating an improved procedure in teaching and learning situations. Pupils differ from each other in numerous ways and adequate provision must be made to assist each in achieving as well as possible.

The Teacher, Reading and the Pupil

A big book procedure has many strengths. Here in a small group of six or seven learners, the teacher must have a large book for all to see clearly. The chosen library book should contain illustrations to assist in making the print more meaningful for pupils. Interest in reading materials is a prime factor in the selection of library books. The library book should also be on the understanding level of pupils and avoid overly complex or too simplistic reading materials. The teacher discusses the illustrations and reads aloud the content the first time and observes pupils to see they follow along with the printed words. Next, the pupils read aloud together with the teacher. In this way, pupils need not stumble on unknown words but may focus on interesting ideas instead. With the read aloud, pupils may develop a basic sight vocabulary. In the third oral reading, pupils may read independently. Involved learners can then read independently. Pupils might then discuss the contents for comprehension. There are basically no interruptions in hesitating or in failure to recognize unknown words. Interruptions when viewing unknown words hinder fluency in reading and a lack of skill in word identification.

The teacher may wish to bring in some phonics such as asking pupils the following:

- is there a word, for example which begins like "cat" in the read aloud?
- is there a word which ends like "dog"?
- which word rhymes with "pen"?

Each of the above may be printed on the white board as given by pupils. Activities such as these sharpen learner abilities to transfer word recognition skills to new situations (Ediger, 2008).

Second, basal readers, published by a leading publishing company and adopted by the local school district, is another approach used in teaching reading. The accompanying Manual to the basal readers provides assistance to the teacher to determine objectives for pupil attainment, learning opportunities to achieve these objectives and appraisal techniques to evaluate learner progress. These three items in curriculum development may be modified in the teaching and learning process, as needed. Thus, basal readers may be used in a formal manner as prescribed in the Manual, or used flexibly as needed to provide for individual differences.

The stories have been chosen by specialists in the field of reading. The Manual section, too, has been developed by reading specialists. They will emphasize, among other things, phonics, word attack skills, and different comprehension strategies to use in teaching. The chosen stories may not reflect the interests of learners, but ways of motivating pupils to enjoy the diverse stories is stressed. The Manual section does provide assistance to teachers in teaching if used informally to provide for the needs of learners (See McConachie, *et al.*, 2006).

Third, programmed readers use a carefully structured sequence whereby pupils make few errors in reading. This is especially true if the program has been field tested. Thus, in programmed reading the sequence moves forward very slowly into gradually more complex learnings. Thus on the monitor, the pupil may read a sentence or more, for example and then respond to a multiple choice test item to notice pupil under-standing. The correct answer then is provided. If the pupil was correct in responding, he/she is rewarded. If incorrect, the pupil still will go in to the next programmed item. Read, respond, check is used consistently in having pupils move forward in programmed. Programmers write the complete programme of reading instruction which consists of objectives, programmed learning opportunities and appraisal techniques consisting of answers to each item (See Liang and Dole, 2006).

A fourth instructional plan involves individualized reading. A set of quality library books is placed at a centre for pupils to browse through and then each chooses a book to read. The individual pupil will choose a book of personal interest to read. He/she completes reading the entire book and then has a conference with the teacher. At the conference, comprehension will be evaluated through a discussion of library book content. The pupils is asked to read a selection from the library book to appraise fluency in reading. Notes are written and dated in order to refer to for the next conference when a completed library book has been read. Progress may be noted when making comparisons in pupil progress (See Carlsen and Sherill, 1988).

Fifth, peer reading involves three or four peers taking turns reading aloud a chosen book. Guidelines are adhered to in cooperative learning endeavors. Assistance is provided in reading by peers as needed. A discussion follows of the content read with higher levels of cognition stressed. The teacher supervises the discussion. Peer teaching may be emphasized to assist in word recognition as well as in comprehension strategies. Independence in reading is stressed in small groups achieving objectives of instruction. For all reading experiences, pupils my extend learnings through a variety of activities such as creative dramatics (See Bolton and Heathcote, 1995).

Sixth, after initial learnings have been achieved as in phonics and word recognition together with a basic sight vocabulary, linguistic procedures might be stressed in teaching pupils to advance in reading. It then is not necessary to view each word analytically, but the context of the reading material keeps the reader on track. Thus with sequentially reading a selection, the pupil will notice if he/she is or is not comprehending ideas contextually. A good reader then reads fluently and notices if he/she is on track. If the reader has strayed a little from the ideas presented by the writer, sequential ideas will lead to a corrected course (See Goodman, 1996).

Seventh, the experience chart approach stresses a concrete/semi-concrete to abstract order of experiences. Thus, a set of pupils, for example, view and discuss a set of objects on an interest center. In sequence, the learners provide information, orally, on what was observed for the teacher to record on a chalkboard as the sentences are given. As each sentence is given slowly, pupils see talk written down. Pupils then with teacher guidance read aloud the entire printed content as the teacher points to each word in sequence. Pupils may reread the content until mastered or before interest wanes. Here, pupils do not face difficulties in word recognition. The teacher together with pupils read the subject matter aloud, followed by learners independently doing the reading as the teacher points to each word while it is being read. Ideas read are meaningful since pupils observed and discussed real objects, previously, at a learning center. This is a cooperative endeavor since pupils and the teacher worked together, harmoniously, to develop the experience chart (Ediger, 2006).

Eighth, a patterns approach is stressed in spelling which has tremendous implications for reading instruction. Thus in a basal spelling textbook, words for pupil mastery in a lesson, for example, might consist of the "man" pattern of words in a family: ban, can, fan, pan, among others. By changing an initial consonant in this case, pupils come up with a new word. Other word patterns may include the following:

- words ending in the suffix "ing".
- words containing a prefix, *e.g.* "un".
- words beginning with a selected letter, *e.g.* "i" as in lion, lamb, lonesome
- words ending with a certain letter, such as "p", as in the words mop, pop, top
- shorter words being inherent in longer words.

By noticing patterns in spelling words, pupils possess clues in word recognition. Certain patterns are repetitive and transfer to the identification of other words (Ediger 2008).

Ninth, sustained silent reading (SSR) is a plan of reading whereby the pupil chooses a library book of his own liking to read silently. A special time is devoted during the school day for SSR. Pupils tend to select books on their own individual reading level so that meaning is attached to the activity. They also tend to choose library books of personal interest and worth. The purpose of SSR is to encourage reading time. Learners then practice the act of reading independently. The teacher monitors SSR to make sure that each child has selected a library book and is actively involved in reading. Generally, there is no direct teaching and no formal evaluation of reading progress here, except that the teacher observes involved pupils being actively involved in silent reading. SSR does give pupils time to engage in decision making and taking responsibility for reading.

Tenth, the Great Books organization has much to offer pupils. Initially, the Great Books organization stressed the importance of pupils reading and enjoying the classics. Classical literature, in many cases, is too complex for elementary and middle school students. However, *Classics Illustrated,* for example, written in comic book form simplified the content of the Great Books. With large pictures and simplified accompanying print, many pupils tended to enjoy reading the content pertaining to Tom Sawyer, Huckleberry Finn, the House of Seven Gables, among others. Looking at the opposite side of the coin, there are experts who recommend that the classics be read in their original form at the high school and university level. The Great Books presently recommends that a class of pupils with teacher guidance choose a well written library book on the developmental level of children and cooperatively explore its contents in a stimulating manner. The purpose here is for pupils to read and enjoy good literature.

In Conclusion

There are a plethora of plans in the teaching of reading. Each has its own unique appeal. Teachers and school administrators need to study indepth each plan and come up with the best in aiding pupils to achieve in reading. Perhaps, with a combination of ideas from the diverse plans, pupils may be assisted to gain in reading skills and thus increase comprehension to include critical and creative thinking, as well as problem solving skills.

REFERENCES

Bolton, G. and D. Hearthecote (1995), *Drama for Learning.* Portsmouth, New Hampshire: Heinemann.

Carlsen, G. R. and A. Sherrill (1988), *Readers: How We Come to Love Books.* Urbana, Illinois: National Council Teachers of English.

Ediger, Marlow (2008), "Psychology of Parental Involvement in Reading," *Reading Improvement*, 45 (1), 46-52.

Ediger, Marlow (2006), "Administration of Schools," *College Student Journal*, 40(4), 846-851.

Ediger, Marlow (2008), "The Principal in the Teaching and Learning Process," *Education*, 129 (4), 574-578.

Goodman, Y. (1996), "Reevaluating Readers While Readers Revalue Themselves; Retrospective Miscue Analyses," *The Reading Teacher*, 19 (8), 600-615.

Liang, Lauren Aimonette and Janice Dole (2006), "Help with Teaching Reading Comprehension: Comprehending Instructional Frameworks," *The Reading Teacher*, 59 (8).

McConachie (2006), "Task, Text and Talk: Literacy for all Subjects," *Educational Leadership*, 64 (2), 8-15.

Data-based Instruction in Reading

Data-based instruction has received much attention in educational literature. It relates well to measurement driven teaching and learning. Data may come from several sources including mandated tests, district wide testing, formative and summative evaluations, as well as teacher written tests.

Objective information is intended for use in data based strategy of teaching and learning. Information secured from pupil test results deemed objective measurements provide teachers needed information in assisting pupils to achieve well.

Data-based Reading Instruction

Data from test results provide objectives for instruction. Machine scoring is generally used; however in the case of teacher written tests, hand scoring may be more convenient. From computer printouts, the teacher has knowledge of what pupils missed and what is left to learn. Learning activities, aligned with these objectives, help learners to achieve the precise objectives. Objectives must be stated with precision so that little/no leeway exists for their interpretation. It must be measurable if the objectives have/have not been achieved after instruction. Individual differences need to be provided for since achievement levels from test results will vary (Ediger, 2009).

With mandated testing in the different states, many are using standardized tests, already published, or have been designed for a state to harmonize with stated, specific objectives of instruction. The standardized tests generally have been pilot tested in a representative sampling of students. Standardized means that those taking the test receive the same test items for their age or grade level, the directions given are the same, as are the time limits for test taking. The tests are valid if they measure what is purported to be evaluated, such as a test measuring pupil achievement in word recognition, measure something different such as grammar, syntax and semantics. If the standardized test is based on knowledge of grammar, then this is what needs to be tested in order to be valid.

Equally salient as compared to validity is the concept of reliability. Thus, a test needs to measure consistently with either test/retest, split half, and/or alternate forms reliability. The Manual accompanying the standardized test provides information on validity and how it was ascertained as well as reliability data. Pupil test results are then compared from the given standardized test to pilot tested information contained in the Manual. Student test results will be given in percentiles, generally, but also might include grade equivalent, age equivalent, and stanine scores. Thus, a student may be on the forty-fifth percentile, based on others who had taken the same test in the pilot studies representing the norms contained in the Manual (Ediger, 2008).

There are standardized tests in reading which cover a plethora of objectives such as reading comprehension in general, critical reading, problem solving, creative reading, phonics skills, and word recognition, among others. Useful information about pupils may be attained if these tests possess high validity as well as reliability. Standardized test then provide information in data driven decision-making.

Standardized tests are given once in a school year and thus do not provide data on pupil achievement during each day of the school year. Teacher written tests then also become salient. Multiple choice tests written by classroom teachers need to follow quality standards of writing test items and these include the following:

- each of the four distractors must be plausible. An unreasonable distractor may be immediately eliminated by the pupil. Thus, fewer than four distractors provide more opportunities for guessing the correct response of a multiple choice test item.
- the four distractors need to be of similar length so as not to provide clues as to which is correct.
- each distractor must be grammatically correct with the stem. This also minimizes chances for guessing the correct response. Selected teacher written test items may have no stem, *e.g.* which of the following words is spelled incorrectly:

  (*a*) manager (*b*) sincerely (*c*) lumber (*d*) ample.

  * face validity needs to be used in that the teacher writes the test items which cover what has been taught.
  * the test must be written on the developmental level of learners (Ediger, 2008).

True/false teacher written tests have merit if quality test writing is involved and pupils need to correct the part of a test item, if it is incorrect. Securing the correct answer is a 50 per cent possibility unless the pupil must correct the incorrect part of a test item. Notice the following incorrectly written true/false test item:

The following words represent alliteration—pizza, pie, put, sell. The word "sell" is incorrect since it does not begin with the same sound as the others.

Matching tests may be beneficial to measure pupil knowledge of vital facts. There needs to be more items in one column as compared to the other so that the process of elimination is minimized. Column A is then matched with items in column B. Lengthy sentences should not be written for each column since it becomes difficult to keep all the information in mind for matching purposes. Thus in column A, important concepts may be written such as synonyms; antonyms; acronyms; metaphors; hyperbole, slang; idioms;

oxymoron; personification; homophones. Column B contains brief definitions for matching with the correct concept in column A (See Baumann, *et al.*, 2007).

Each kind of teacher written test should provide feedback to both teachers and pupils as to what needs more emphasis in teaching and learning situations. Test data should inform which objectives need more stress in the curriculum.

Essay tests might well provide much information on pupil progress in an ongoing lesson/unit of study. These tests must have questions which are not factual, nor do they require a chapter in their writing. Pupil written responses may be assessed using a quality rubric to insure more objective grading. Thus, the following need appraisal:

- analysis, synthesis, and evaluation in the written product, depending upon which are valid for testing
- use of complete sentences
- clarity of ideas expressed
- correct grammar and spelling of words.

The following are examples of essay test items:

- Take a character from any story studied and change him/her into a different being which fits into that story setting.
- Why do you think the actual character in a different story chose his/her future as was done?
- Write a summary of the setting of different stories studied in the just completed unit of study (See Almasi, 2003).

In writing any kind of test item age/grade, and ability levels of learners must be taken into thorough consideration. The use of precise objectives works well with data driven decision making since clarity of information is desired from pupils as a result of the latter experiencing appropriate learning activities. The learning activities must be aligned with the stated objectives. This makes it possible to secured data from assessment results, which in turn, drives instruction (See Pettyjohn and Sacco, 2007).

Contrasting Data Driven Decision with Constructivism

Constructivism uses other procedures of in teaching to secure information on pupil progress than testing. With constructivism, the following, among others, are salient:

- teacher observation of pupils in every day lessons when the latter learn by discovery. Testing is minimized.
- pupil self-evaluation with teacher guidance.
- the teacher assists pupils in specific learning opportunities to reflect upon difficulties and come up with a satisfactory answer.
- pupil interests, questions, and feelings become a part of ongoing units of study.
- learning is social and small group endeavors are important in discussing content (See Vygotsky, 1978).

REFERENCES

Almasi, J. (2003), *Teaching Specific Processes in Reading*. New York: Guilford.

Baumann, James F. *et al*., (2007), "Bumping into Spicy, Testy Words That Catch Your Tongue." A Formative Experiment in Vocabulary Instruction," *The Reading Teacher*, 61 (2), 108-122.

Ediger, Marlow (2008), Leadership in the School Setting," *Education, 129* (1), 17-20.

Ediger, Marlow (2008), "The American High School," *College Student Journal*, 42(3), 814-817.

Ediger, Marlow (2009), "For an Effective Reading Program," *Reading Improvement*, 46(3), 119-122.

Pettyjohn, Terry F. and Matthew F. Sacco (2007), "Multiple-Choice Exam Questions". Order Influence on Student Performance, Completion Time, and Performance," *Journal of Instructional Psychology*, 34 (3), 142-149.

Vygotsky, L. S. (1978), *Mind in Society: The Development of Higher Psychological Processes*. Cambridge, MA.: Harvard University Press.

Teaching Reading and the Common Core Standards

The common core standards emphasize a kindergarten through secondary school progression and will apply to all students in the nation. National tests then measure pupil progress. They are different from the No Child Left Behind (NCLB) law in that the latter stressed that each state develop their own tests to measure pupil achievement, making it impossible to notice how well pupils did nationally. NCLB then emphasized ascertaining pupil progress based on separate tests for states individually. Thus, one state may have easier or more complex tests than did the other(s).

The question arises, "How might learner attainment be optimized in reading?"

Motivating Common Core Learning

Pupils need motivation to achieve needed knowledge and skills in reading. For young children, the following word attack skills need mastering:

- using picture clues, as well as selected learnings in phonics as in initial consonants to recognize words
- context clues, patterns in words and syllabication analysis as needed.

Comprehension of subject matter should include obtaining main ideas and subordinating content, cause and effect thinking; identification of characters, the setting of the narrative, the sequence of the action and the plot.

The above word recognition skills as well as comprehension strategies serve as a basis for future success in reading and in attaining common core objectives. Each ensuing objective builds upon previous learnings. Background information is needed in subject matter as well as in skills to achieve as optimally as possible in acquiring progression in reading. The new objective must be attained as seamlessly as possible when relating the new with previously achieved objectives. Additional objectives which need attention include the following as learners achieve progress throughout the school year:

- critical reading in separating facts from opinions, accurate content from the inaccurate, and fantasy from reality.
- creative reading in coming up with novel ideas, uniqueness of thought, and originality.
- problem solving strategies whereby the reader generalizes from data given in answer to a dilemma situation.
- reading to attain vital concepts.
- reading between the lines.
- reading directions to develop a project in an ongoing unit of study.

Reading should be a useful and a practical curriculum area in school and in society and in attaining common core objectives. Classroom teachers must provide ample time for silent as well as oral reading. In oral reading, teachers may discern the kinds of errors made by individual pupils. These might well become a basis for instruction in small and large groups if they are somewhat persistent to most learners. Otherwise individual assistance might well be given as the oral reading progresses. Errors (miscues) may consist of not being able to identify a word, giving an incorrect substitution, hesitating in word recognition, lacking fluency in reading, omitting words, among others. Each miscue needs identification and remedied with patience as well as quality instruction.

Silent reading should be stressed during reading instruction as well as in sustained silent reading. The latter emphasizes each pupil choosing a library book to read toward completion. If a pupil is not able to settle down with reading a library book, the teacher may suggest one which harmonizes with that pupil's interests, and achievement level. Periodically, a conference may be held with the reader to appraise skills in word recognition and in comprehension. The point being that children need to read library books at home and in school. They become good readers through reading which help in word identification as well as in comprehension. The home setting can do much to aid in the goal of reading progress by reading aloud with enthusiasm to offspring and providing honest praise for effort put forth by children. A variety of library books should be available to children in the home setting. These may be purchased and/or secured from the public library.

Being a good reader is necessary in school and in society, at the work place. Well paying and responsible jobs/ professions require high quality abilities in reading. Throughout the secondary school years, more reading of abstract materials is emphasized; thus reading readiness needs to be sequential from the elementary school years and upward. Thus, students need to hone skills in critical and creative reading, reflective thought, problem solving, as well as reading analytically. Self-efficacy is highly significant in that the student feels confident to face tasks of the future. Leaning upon the self and engaging in quality decisions making abilities is salient.

To engage in more complex skills in reading, high school students need to have ample opportunities to engage in the following, among others:

- reading for a variety of purposes in classes taken in different curriculum/academic disciplines.
- taking part in and writing school plays and in reader's theater.
- doing much writing, directly related to course work, and proofing of written work.

- writing poems for publication with assistance provided by consultant teachers.
- being a member of the school newspaper writing team.
- increased reading for leisure and enjoyment.

Common Core Objectives can be achieved with a high quality schedule in reading.

The amount of reading done on the higher education level is indeed great. It is amazing in selected college/university courses that a student is able to complete all the complex reading required in a semester! It must be a major objectives of all teachers/instructors to stress the saliency of reading. All teachers need to be teachers of reading regardless of the title of the course taught. For those attending technical school, reading skills are vital in all endeavors of work. The writer, for example, when attending a rural high school, 1942-1946, engaged in much reading when taking three years of vocational agriculture. These were good experiences for one who is highly academic, being vice president and president of the local FFA Chapter, being third high in the state FFA livestock judging contest, as well as being awarded the State Farmer degree open to two per cent of the members within the state. Perceiving the saliency of reading in all of life's endeavors assists in attaining common core objectives.

Writing Across the Curriculum

To often, classroom teachers wish to separate writing into a separate component apart from the rest of the curriculum. Thus, little emphasis is placed upon assisting pupils to integrate written work in science, mathematics, social studies, and literature, as well as its use in society. Writing is an essential skill which cuts across daily activities performed by individuals. Much effort, time and practice must be put into written work and its saliency. Well planned lessons consisting of vital objectives, learning experiences and appraisal procedures need to be in the offing. Learners need to be motivated to be wholeheartedly involved in writing across the curriculum (Ediger, 2007).

Pointers in Teaching Writing

There are salient objectives to emphasize in composition and written work. First, pupils must be actively involved in doing written work. If pupils are not involved, the chances are that slovenly products may accrue. Interest is a powerful factor in writing, and the language arts teachers must select those experiences which enrich and assist pupils to possess an inward desire to write. This might emphasize pupils participating individually or collectively in writing poetry, short stories, reader's theater, plays, persuasive essays, sympathy notes, word problems in mathematics, and summaries, among others, in ongoing lessons and units of study. Actual scenes in the out of doors as well as objects and items in the classroom, might stimulate writing when perceived in an ongoing discussion. Concrete situations are then stressed in written work; the semi-concrete may also provide subject matter for waiting such as illustrations, slides in power point presentations, as well as the pictorial observed on the internet including scenes pertaining to current events. Pupils with teacher guidance need to explore different content sources for learner engagement in writing across the curriculum.

Second, pupils must perceive purpose in writing across the curriculum. Reasons are then accepted by pupils to participate in ongoing experiences. Frequently, learners think of writing activities as busy work, and behave accordingly. If learners, for example, are to write an actual invitation for parents to come to the annual open house event, then a purpose for writing is involved. Technology such as the word processor might well be utilized in the written work. There are a plethora of lifelike activities which pupils may participate in when writing across the curriculum such as writing business and friendly letters, summaries, diary entries, and journal writing (Ediger and Rao, 2003), among others. The goal is to have pupils engage in writing and thus improve in its clarity, grammar, and usage.

Third, pupils need to experience an environment conducive to writing. The environment is free from rudeness, negative comments, put downs, as well as comments which hinder goal attainment in writing across the curriculum. Rather, collaboration or individual endeavors involve good public relations among pupils (see Vygotsky, 1934-1986).

Fourth, individual differences must be provided for in writing across the curriculum. Selected learners will need more assistance than others. The subject matter inherent in written work comes first in importance as it must contain important ideas, not trivia, nor the routine. Rather, the focal point is upon rich ideas which fascinate the writer as well as the audience. Grammar becomes salient as it assists in writing meaningful content. Thus, agreement of subject and predicate, correct tense of verbs, as well as modifiers placed properly, among other items, may need attention as they enhance the subject matter in the written work.

Fifth, learning styles differ among pupils in the classroom. Thus, there are preferences in how pupils process information. The following procedures of teaching provide for differences in styles of learning:

- rather heavy use of basal textbooks and accompanying workbooks versus an activity centred approach.
- project methods of instruction whereby learners have considerable input into the learning sequence.
- problem solving procedures in which writing across the curriculum is emphasized in answer to a question or problem.
- learning experiences to attain predetermined objectives as in a mandated curriculum.
- independent or small group activities whereby individual needs differ as ongoing lessons and units indicate.

Conclusion

Language arts in writing across the curriculum provide pupils with a plethora of activities and experiences. Each pupil must attain optimally in a rich, high quality curriculum to do well in school and in society. The best of objectives, learning experiences, as well as appraisal procedures (valid and reliable), must be in the offing.

REFERENCES

Ediger, Marlow (2007), "Learning Activities in the Curriculum," *College Student Journal*, 41 (4), 967-969.

Ediger, Marlow, and D. Bhaskara Rao (2003), *Teaching Language Arts Successfully*. New Delhi, India: Discovery Publishing House Ltd.

Vygotsky, Len (1934, 1986), *Thought and Language*. Cambridge, Massachusetts, MIT.

The Teaching of Science

There are selected guidelines which are recommended in teaching science. These guidelines assist teachers in promoting learner achievement. First, pupils need to be engaged in ongoing lessons and units of study. This empathizes securing pupil interests. If pupils are not engaged, the chances are that more optimal achievement is not possible. A stimulating environment which captures learner attention is a must. Thus, in performing a science experiment, all pupils involved need to see the experiment clearly. They need to hypothesize as to its outcomes. The writer when supervising university student teachers in the public schools has noticed rather consistently how pupils' attention is drawn to a carefully planned experiment in science with recored learner hypotheses. There is much excitement as to what will transpire. Pupils pay careful attention to the experiment as it actually occurs. Equally exciting is for pupils to keep in mind during experimentation how each hypothesis relates to the ongoing experiment. Objective evidence is wanted to confirm or refute any hypothesis. Jumping to hasty conclusions must be avoided by learners and the teacher.

Second, meaning must be attached by learners to each concept and generalization being stressed. Failure to make sense of new learnings makes for difficulty to add understand content in ensuing lessons being emphasized. For each new concept in ongoing lessons, pupils need indepth learning from a variety of reference sources used to secure knowledge and skills. Indepth learnings assists pupils to build on these ideas for sequential subject matter emphasized.

Third, pupils should experience purpose in learning. With accepted purpose, pupils feel there are reasons for achieving and developing. Relevance in subject matter acquired in science stresses that vital facts, meanings, as well as main ideas can be used in school and in society. In reading science content from a basal textbook to check conclusions drawn from an experiment, pupils need to perceive purpose or reasons for these learnings. The teacher may state the purpose deductively or pupils may be asked questions to arrive at the reasons for reading inductively. Pupils may need assistance in the following when reading science subject matter:

- using context clues to identify unknown words:
- establishing purposes for reading such as reading to secure a main idea or for reading critically and creatively.
- summarizing information gleaned.
- securing information related to a science experiment.
- obtaining background information to do a project or to engage in problem solving.

Fourth, pupils achieve at different levels in science and provision must be made for each to achieve as optimally as possible. Diverse teaching materials related to vital science objectives of instruction need to be in the offing. Concrete, semi-concrete, as well as abstract materials of instruction used judiciously by the teacher should assist pupils to do well in science lessons and units of study. Learnings need to be adapted to the present achievement level of learners with quality ordered activities following. Generally, pupils need to learn inductively through inquiry methods. A multi-cultural environment for learning needs emphasis whereby pupils learn in an atmosphere of respect and acceptance.

Fifth, learning styles of individual pupils must be respected. Thus, selected pupils learn best in a cooperative learning setting whereas others do better on individual projects and activities. However, it is good for all to learn to work together harmoniously since schooling involves a social situation and pupils also must learn to work together in society. At the same time, pupils individually need to be responsible for finding worthwhile tasks during spare time in school and in society.

Chapter 15 Current Events in Ongoing Science Lessons and Units of Study

Current events in science assist pupils to stay abreast of today's happenings. In a democracy it is very salient for all to be well informed of transpiring events. Science in the news helps pupils to understand what is happening in local, state, national, and international events. Pupils need to connect with these happenings as well as attach meaning to diverse occurrences. Ill-informed persons lose out on how science is involved in current events. The science teacher must guide learners to perceive purpose in vital happenings which transpire. Reasons then exist for indepth learning into causes of current happenings on the planet earth. Most current events items deal with the natural environment. These include the following natural disasters:

* mudslides which may devour entire villages and cities.
* forest fires caused by lightning and other natural occurrences which destroy an entire area of farm crops, homes and other buildings.
* earthquakes which weaken or demolish villages, huts and stronger buildings, roads and bridges.
* volcanic eruptions which bury what is in its way and cause panic.
* hail which weakens or eliminates agricultural production as well as causes severe losses/damage to different kinds of structures.

* Tornados which can wipe out a complete city as well as wind power to lift huge trucks into the air.
* Tsunamis with it destructible force of flood waters following an underwater earthquake.

Learning Opportunities

To understand each of the above asterisked current events items, pupils need to experience a variety of developmentally appropriate activities. Each happening needs to be pinpointed on a map and globe. Thus, printouts of illustrations from the internet need to be in the offing for study. Additional illustrations to be discussed in depth might well come from the following reference sources:

- a power point presentation showing a sequence of happenings as in a mudslide.
- pictures from a basal science textbook indicating destructive forces of forest fires.
- illustrations from science encyclopedias on faults, folding, and earthquakes.
- teacher and pupil made models pertaining to volcanos.
- newspaper illustrations and accounts of hail and its effects on farm crops and buildings.
- scenes from newsmagazines showing the power of hurricanes, Tornados and cyclones.
- listening to TV and radio news accounts on the effect of Tsunamis in different regions.

There are several methods to emphasize in organizing the science current events program. One approach is to relate the happening to an ongoing science unit of study. This has its merits since it integrates and indicates relationships of what is being studied. This procedure views subject matter holistically, not in separate parts. Pupils tend to remember content studied better if the new learnings are related to those previously studied. Sequence is then in evidence and resides in the minds of learners. The science teacher might then ascertain at which point in the science curriculum it would be best for current events instruction. In a science unit on "The Changing Surface of the Earth," the concept of *mudslides* may be stressed at the time this concept is being studied. There is then a gradual transition from what is generally taught in the science unit to incorporating the new learning.

A second procedure in teaching science current event is to bring the happening for attention, regardless of it relationship to an ongoing science unit of study. This is done when a relevant happening is unrelated to what is presently being studied in a science unit of study. There are a plethora of current happenings which are unrelated to the present science unit of study being emphasized. Relevancy in the news then indicates there is a need, for example, to report on *forest fires* even though the present unit of study cannot be related to that concept.

Third, the current events concept may be unrelated to the current unit being studied, but may be broadened to become an entire science unit of study. Thus the concept *earthquakes* may be highly important in the news since many regions are experiencing this science phenomenon in different, salient locations on the planet earth. It takes time and quality teaching to assist pupils to understand earthquakes and their after effects in depth. Objectives, learning opportunities, and evaluation procedures may then be developed to teach a developmentally appropriate science unit of study, based on a vital current happening.

Fourth, the integrated current events unit of study may be taught emphasizing science as an academic area largely. Thus in a unit on *hurricanes and tornados,* the following academic disciplines in science may be stressed: earth sciences, physics with its resulting forces in bringing about destructive effects, and biology with its effects on plants and animals. To integrate science and current events with the social studies, among other academic disciplines, the following emphases may be included:

- aid and assistance provided by different relief agencies to minimize pain and suffering.

- the history of major hurricanes on the planet earth and why they occur.
- geographical regions where major hurricanes and tornados transpired.
- assistance provided from different private and governmental agencies to clean up and rebuild an area.

A quality science current events program advocates that teachers follow selected criteria to optimize pupil learning. Thus, pupils need to:

- attach meaning and understanding pertaining to teaching and learning situations.
- be actively involved in learning and participate fully in discussing science current events items.
- perceive purpose in being engaged in achieving vital objectives.
- experience intrinsic sequence as well as perceive subject matter as being related.
- do critical and creative thinking as well as problem solving.

In closing, pupils must experience quality objectives, engaging learning opportunities for pupils to achieve these objectives, and valid/reliable evaluation procedures to notice learner progress.

Meaning in the Science Curriculum

The science teacher has a salient responsibility in assisting pupils to develop meaningful learnings. Too frequently, quickly covering the contents in a basal textbook is stressed without making certain that learners understand what is taught. Pupils need to attach meaning to each concept and generalization taught. Otherwise, pupils will be hindered in understanding subsequent subject matter. An important strategy in teaching is to help pupils attain adequate background information before proceeding with new objectives of instruction. Background information may be secured with the use of authentic content, vicarious experiences, and printed materials. Pupils need to experience developmentally appropriate learning opportunities in order to achieve, accomplish, and grow.

Meaning, Teaching and Learning in Science

Background information, activated with teacher assistance, needs to relate to previous learner experiences. Thus, the pupil connects the old with the new science subject matter. This connection is vital in order to attach meaning to ongoing facts, concepts, and generalizations in each lessons and unit of study. Sequence resides in the minds of pupils and must be planned within this framework. To activate background knowledge, the teacher needs to help pupils to review previously acquired ideas. Thus if pupils are studying Animals with Backbones, they may experience a review of amphibians, going through the stages of egg, tadpoles and the adult state of frog. This can be experienced through illustrations, printouts from the computer and power point presentations. Learners must feel free to ask questions and obtain answers to fill gaps in knowledge (Ediger and Rao, 2007).

To connect with the new subject matter, pupils might well be studying how frogs are a part of the ecology in the natural environment. Interaction with other amphibians and animals with/without backbones, as well as plant life must be studied. Indepth learning emphasizes that the teacher use a variety of kinds of concrete, semi-concrete, as well as abstract activities. In this way, pupils may attach meaning to ongoing experiences.

Also to achieve new objectives, pupils must perceive purpose in learning. Reasons are then accepted for achieving/ learning new subject matter. Pupils, in many situations, do not learn effectively due to having a lack of purpose. The teacher may state and elaborate on the purpose such as, "Today we are going to study some possible reasons for the frog population dwindling in numbers and how this affects the environment." Pupils may also hypothesize why it is poignant to learn about frogs and other animals in the ecological setting. Intrinsically, pupils may then perceive reasons for wholehearted invovlement. Terminology must be used which pupils understand. Meaning theory is always salient in teaching and learning situations. It assists pupils to achieve new, related objectives of instruction; otherwise, pupils might become bored with a lack of challenge. Or, learners may be frustrated if the new learnings are too advanced and unrelated to those acquired previously (See Jackson, *et al.*, 2008).

Interest factors in learning assist pupils to accept reasons for participating wholeheartedly in ongoing science lessons and units of study. Stimulating methods of having pupils learn by discovery can be exciting. This is opposite of being told or lectured on subject matter to be learned. There are science teachers who use a seamless learning by discovery procedure of instruction. At a National Science Teachers Association

Convention, a high school physics instructor remarked that he never responded with answers to questions, raised by students. Instead, he lead them to correct answers with a series of ordered questions. Thinking is a major objective here (See Ritchart and Perkins, 2008).

Interest is also encouraged within engaging learning opportunities. A classroom which emphasizes continuous learning is salient such as in the late spring months having a jar of eggs/tadpoles swimming in water for pupil observation. As these are observed, pupils ask questions of each other and of the teacher pertaining to the phenomenon involved. The identified questions set the stage for problem solving. Different reference sources may be used to secure necessary information. Committees might be formed to attain information with the science teacher serving as a guide and helper. Each committee needs to respect contributions from its members, stay on the topic being pursued, keep the activity moving forward, develop conclusions, and present its findings to other committees. Findings may be shown with the project method whereby a product is completed, which meet the following standards:

- careful planning of the project
- all committee members being actively involved in doing the project
- neatness in the final pursued project.

The writer when supervising university student teachers observed many pupils who truly were interested in the project method and attained major science concepts and generalizations as well as being able to work together. They appeared to work together well in an atmosphere of respect. Pupils tend to understand science subject matter with a hands on approach much better than a lecture/heavy explanation approach (See Dewey, 1916).

Frogs, as well as other vertebrates, live in an environment which includes plant life. To show how significant sunlight is to different plants, the teacher may provide spinach seeds to be seeded properly in small pots. The seed is the same kind for each of two pots with similar soil, as well as needed moisture. One pot receives adequate sunshine after the plants appear above ground; the other is covered with a paper sack. Pupils may then hypothesize and check the hypothesis by observing how appropriate sunlight affects plant growth. The experiment may be replicated if necessary. The amount of moisture might also be checked as a variable in promoting plant growth, with all other conditions kept constant including quality of seed, sunlight and soil. Experiments conducted need to be on the understanding level of learners so that meaningful learnings accrue. They must be clearly visible to all participants. Careful observations, here, by pupils is salient. Hypotheses need to be recorded in order to test each (See American Association for the Advancement of Science, 1989).

Pupils need to be able to read well from basal science textbooks, internet sources, as well as library books among others; selected hypotheses might well be checked through reading. Meaningful reading might be achieved, using the following recommended methodology, with pupils developing/using:

- context clues to ascertain unknown words in context.
- analytical procedures in word recognition such as phonetic analysis, syllabication skills and dividing a word into prefixes and suffixes.
- main ideas, subordinate content, and details, related, in reading science subject matter.
- critical reading (separating facts from opinions, fantasy from reality, as well as accurate from inaccurate statements), creative reading (developing new, original ideas and ways of pursing a goal) and problem solve.
- evaluative procedures in appraising the worth of subject matter read for purposeful activities (See National Research Council, 1996).

Current Events in Science Units and Lessons

With a quality current events program, the teacher develops and maintains an updated science program. There are a plethora of current happenings which affect people around the world. Pupils must understand why these happenings occur in nature. Causes and effects need to be studied. Meaning needs to be attached to these learnings. Common occurrences in natural disasters include the following and need to be included in a developmental current events curriculum in science:

- floods, mud slides and soil erosion.
- tornados and hurricanes which also cause heavy property loss.
- volcanic eruptions.
- forest fires, draught and water shortages.

Pupils need to study each of the above meaningfully and understand what can be done to alleviate human suffering from these occurrences. Diverse organizations and volunteers which provide assistance must be studied.

There are numerous things done to make for a cleaner environment as well as save energy costs. These include:

- use of wind energy such as windmills
- utilization of solar energy including solar panels on homes
- updating appliances to make for more energy efficiency
- use of ethanol instead of gasoline and diesel fuel to power vehicles
- insulating houses to preserve energy used in summer and winter
- having plants indoors to minimize the effects of carbon dioxide (Ediger, 2009).

Pupils must understand why it is salient to conserve energy and how each of the above assists in conservation methods as well as provide for a cleaner environment. The list may well be extended by pupils with teacher guidance. Direct observation should be made by pupils of these endeavors, whenever possible.

REFERENCES

American Association for the Advancement of Science (1989), *Benchmarks for Science Literacy*. New York: Oxford University Press.

Dewey, John (1916), *Democracy and Education*. New York: Macmillan Company.

Ediger, Marlow (2009), "Innovations in Teaching Science," *Connecticut Journal of Science Education*, 47 (2), 27-28.

Ediger, Marlow and D. Bhaskara Rao (2007), School Science Education. New Delhi, India: *Discovery Publishing House Ltd.*

Jackson, Julie, *et al.*, (2008), "Connections Charts and Book Talk Groups," *Science and Children*, 46 (3), 27-31.

National Research Council (1996), *National Science Education Standards*. Washington, DC: National Academy Press.

Ritchart, Ron, and David Perkins (2008), "Making Thinking Visible," *Educational Leadership*, 65 (5), 57-63.

Teaching Science in the School Setting

What makes for high quality teaching in ongoing lessons and units of study? Engagement in learning is a key component; learners then need to experience interest in science which the science teacher must attempt to provide for in the curriculum. On task behaviour is salient here in assisting pupils to achieve objectives through carefully planned experiences. Within these learning activities, pupils need to possess high expectations, but still be successful in achievement. Feelings of self-efficacy should result in that learners feel confident in attaining, growing, and accomplishing. There are a plethora of factors then that enter in raising the question, "What makes for a good science curriculum?"

The Science Curriculum, the Pupil and the Teacher

The science teacher must possess breadth and depth of knowledge in science content. Relevant facts, concepts, structural ideas and generalizations enter into the equation. Essential content is very salient for teachers to possess to provide basic learnings to pupils. Along with vital subject matter, challenging and stimulating methods utilized by the science teacher assist learners to attain vital objectives of instruction. Inquiry methods used in ongoing lessons and units of study make it possible to use scientific procedures in knowledge acquisition. Experiments and demonstrations also guide pupils in inquiry procedures and need to be at the heart of science investigations. Technology utilized such as science equipment, online learning and power point presentations help to vary the kinds of activities provided for pupils, as well as provide for active engagement in the curriculum. For all activities, readiness for learning must be there. Thus, pupils have adequate background information and skills to benefit from ensuing lessons and units of study (Ediger and Rao, 2011). Meaning is highly salient for emphasis in teaching and learning situations. Thus, each learner must understand what is being taught. These experiences are the building blocks for achieving new, challenging objectives. Pupil attention will dissipate if meaning and understanding is not present. Their attention will then focus on other things unrelated to what is being studied. Then too, misbehaviour may occur resulting in hindering progress. The writer, when supervising university student teachers, has noticed how pupils have memorized content for a test and yet understanding of ideas was lacking. A key component of learning is attaching meaning to subject matter so that it makes sense.

Pupil purpose is salient in learning. If pupils do not perceive reasons for learning, energy levels tend to go downhill. The science teacher then must guide pupils to see how science subject matter/skills are useful in both school and in society. The science teacher needs to assist pupils in relating what is taught in school to the larger social environment. Sometimes, changing how pupils are grouped for instruction might well help motivate learners. Thus, from large group instruction, the teacher may have pupils work collaboratively. These are small groups of pupils, for example, working harmoniously on solving an identified problem in science. Time also must be given for individual study and project methods of teaching. Thus the learning styles of pupils receive attention with pupils experiencing large group, collaborative, and individual preferences for instructional purposes in science (Searson and Dunn, 2001).

A learning environment is necessary, conducive to pupil progress. The environment needs to stress politeness and acceptance of others. Rudeness and abrupt behaviour must be modified in order to emphasize a classroom atmosphere which facilitates more optimal achievement. Each pupil must be respected as well as he/she respecting the science teacher. The writer believes strongly on working on an environment in the classroom which develops good attitudes as well as aids cognitive attainment. He witnessed in a classroom while supervising university student teachers how misbehaviour truly hindered learner development; pupils in this classroom were learning but the learning was bad behavior rather than achieving objectives of science teaching and learning. The teacher must model and enforce quality behavior as well as being an example in attaining good conduct in the classroom. Higher test scores, too, should then be in the offing, be it on the local, state and/or other levels of mandated standardized tests.

I have in front of me a newspaper headline titled, "More Public Schools Offering Three Meals a Day," which goes on to say, "Too often it is after the fact that teachers discover their students are worrying less about math and reading and more about where the next meal will come from. With breakfast and lunch already provided for poor students, many children now are getting all their meals in school."

When you know about those situations those kids are bringing into the classroom and we are asking them to sit down and concentrate and do their work, and they might be hungry and we haven't been aware of it yet—we definitely want to do everything possible we can to help the kids (Associated Press, The Hutchinson, Kansas News, February 21, 2012).

Poverty is a tremendous problem in society and the public schools, as indicated above, can do much to minimize one problem and that is hunger. They can also do much to provide for belonging needs such as assisting pupils in working together on collaborative endeavours within a wholesome environment. Then too, recognizing pupils as having much worth, as well as when pupils reveal achievement, aids in self esteem needs being met. Thus, pupil achievement can be optimized, numerous ways, in subject matter achievement in the school setting.

Parent/teacher conferences should be held periodically to communicate how well pupils are achieving. A variety of means might well be utilized here, such as e-mail, telephone/cell phone, PTA meetings and conferences in the school setting, among others. Both parents and the teacher must communicate learner achievement in science knowledge and processes, as well as attitudes toward ongoing lessons and units of study. Parents need to be guided in

- assisting pupils in reading library books and other profitable materials in science.
- helping learners understand news items on TV pertaining to the "whys" of earthquakes, tornados, cyclones, tsunamis, mudslides, avalanches, volcanic eruptions, among others.
- involving pupils in problem solving experiences such as analyzing reasons for drought and floods (See, National Research Council, 1996).

Conclusion

Science teachers must choose high quality objectives for learner attainment, relevant activities and experiences for pupil interaction, as well as evaluation procedures to ascertain progress. Evaluation procedures must be varied to embrace approaches including the following:

- valid and reliable testing procedures
- portfolios containing pupil products
- audio/visual recordings of oral reports, committee endeavours and class as a whole participation
- teacher recorded observations made of learners in the school setting
- pupil written products to include the use of word processors, as well as numerous digital/electronic modes.

The atmosphere in the classroom needs to be such that each pupil feels safe and is assisted to achieve as much as possible.

REFERENCES

Associated Press, The Hutchinson, Kansas News, "More Public Schools Offering Three Meals a Day", February 21, 2012, p. 3.

Ediger, Marlow, and D. Bhaskara Rao (2011), *Essays in Teaching Science*. New Delhi, India; Discovery Publishing House Ltd.

National Research Council (1996), National Science Education Standards. Washington, DC: National Academies Press.

Searson, Robert, and Rita Dunn (2001), "The Learning Styles Teaching Model," *Science and Children*, 38 (5), 22-36.

Science and the Common Core State Standards

The common core state standards attempt to prepare a pupil from kindergarten up to college and career readiness. This is quite an undertaking in emphasizing the beginning of public schooling until entering college/career. This covers a fairly long span of years in which the pupil may experience a plethora of changes in life and in society. With continuous change occurring in the societal arena, the science curriculum must also need to change. New technology, inventions and hypotheses accrue in science. Needs in society also change which make for new technology and their application. Nearly all states in the union have signed on to giving the CCSS tests which harmonize with their objectives of instruction. NCLB neglected the science curriculum until 2008 when it was added to the annual test. Teachers are pressured to teach what is on the test and this eliminated several salient academic areas, science included. Science was still minimized in 2008 and succeeding school years due to heavy being emphasis placed upon upping reading and mathematics test scores. CCSS should ameliorate this situation with focus placed upon a broader scope and sequence, including science.

It seems as if No Child Left Behind (NCLB) had just come into being (2002) and it has not been reestablished as of now; however, Congress is not to on and NCLB is still being mandated in school testing situations although a plethora of public schools are receiving waivers to make substitutions as in the Adequate Yearly Progress (AYP) part of NCLB. The standards were set too high in AYR with many schools failing to meet that criterion. With CCSS, it appears that science will again receive its due importance.

Science and its Relevancy

Much is written in educational literature about the need for engineers in society. Thus science educators have advocated a curriculum of Science, Technology, Engineering, and Mathematics (STEM). This should aid in developing a high quality curriculum of science education, kindergarten through grade twelve. A well planned, integrated sequence of subject matter must then be in the offing. The scope of science units need to be broad enough to cover what is deemed needed subject matter to develop a scientific literate person. Teachers need to be properly educated in teaching science on the different grade levels. Elementary school teachers should have at least a minor in science with middle and secondary teachers possessing a major, from an accredited university. Science education should not stop here due to the necessity of upgrading one's own teaching. Thus, inservice education should be continuous and ongoing. Going on for an advance university degree in science teaching/subject matter is salient. The teacher also needs to communicate with other teachers in the school setting about methods of teaching in improving the curriculum. Each public school should have a professional library for teachers which offer the latest science journal articles as well as science teacher education textbooks which offer approaches in upgrading science instruction. The whole point being for science teachers to become enthused and motivated in the professional arenas. In addition, attending professional meetings for science teachers on the state and national levels provide relevant ideas in assisting pupils to achieve more optimally (Ediger artd Rao, 2011). All of these suggestions together with being highly knowledgeable about the CCSS and their implementation once again highlight the saliency of science instruction. Self-efficacy is important for science teachers in that feeling capable in teaching/learning situations is vital in aiding learner achievement and progress. Feelings of capability grow as teachers become more interested and desire to become professional in attitudes, science subject matter, as well as skills in the instructional arenas.

Teachers reflecting upon taught helps to modify what did not work well as well as what was effective. Reflecting does not stress worrying about weaknesses, but upon strengthening the teaching profession. Quality attitudes need development and reinforced in all of life, Pupils, no doubt, view the attitudinal dimension of teachers and might well model their own behaviors in following these criteria.

Methods of teaching need to incorporate how scientists work in their very own fields of endeavor. Quality experiments then must be in the offing as they to the ongoing science units of study. Science experimentation should be a key component of a relevant curriculum. This includes establishing an hypothesis, evaluating the hypothesis, as well as making necessary revisions therein, if necessary. It is good to have an ample supply of commercial science equipment with selected items being in the project by pupils with teacher guidance.

Computers which project large illustrations and subject matter on a white board, along with other updated technology/materials must be an inherent part of a modern science curriculum. Problem solving, critical and creative thinking are needed and necessary ingredients in ongoing science units of study. Individual differences need to be viewed and provisions made for when implementing holism in teaching and learning. Reading materials, be they basal/ electronic textbooks, are to be there for pupils to use in ongoing lessons (Ediger and Rao, 2009). Additional factors in instruction which must be tended to include the following:

- careful, accurate observations made of natural phenomenon
- developing reading skills which encourage quality comprehension, developing accurate conclusions, as welt as synthesizing information gathered

- writing which reflects thoroughness, English but respecting the learner's present achievement level, needed sequence, appropriate syntax, and clarity in semantics
- speaking in a meaningful, coherent manner and yet respecting other dialects
- listening for a variety of purposes in securing vital ideas in science such as facts, concepts, generalizations, as well as answers to questions.

Selected experiences in the classroom should involve collaboration. In and in school, pupils must learn to work harmoniously together. All should participate in the small group with no one dominating and ideas should circulate within the committee, acceptance of other's ideas needs to be forthcoming in an atmosphere of respect. Rudeness in all of its dimensions should be eliminated since It hinders more optima! pupii achievement and progress.

In Conclusion

Utilizing proper procedures in teaching is necessary for pupils to achieve CCSS criteria. Methods of teaching emphasizing scientific inquiry are also relevant in developing science literacy. A classroom and school climate stressing achievement in science is conducive to teaching and learning.

REFERENCES

Ediger, Marlow and D. Bhaskara Rao (2009), *School Science Education*. New Delhi, India: Discovery Publishing House Ltd.

Ediger, Marlow and D. Bhaskara Rao (2011), *Essays in Teaching Science*. New Delhi, India: Discovery Publishing House Ltd.

Pointers in Teaching the Social Studies

Social studies teachers need to follow definite psychological guidelines in teaching and learning situations. When attending to these guidelines, pupil achievement will be more optimal. Which then should be followed in the instructional arena?

First, teachers need to be certain that each pupil is actively involved in ongoing activities. Being inattentive, the pupil does not focus upon the ensuing lesson. With teacher observation, appropriate voice inflection, as well as being well prepared for teaching and learning situations, he/she provides an high quality atmosphere for classroom participation. If this fails to engage learners, then more stimulating experience must be chosen which provide for individual differences (Ediger and Rao, 2007).

Second, pupils need to perceive purpose in learning. Thus, there are good reasons accepted by learners for active participation in ongoing lessons and units of study. Energized pupils feel that it is salient to achieve objectives of study. Purposeless experiences assist in making for lower achievement.

Third, learners must sense sequence in learning in that the ensuing relates directly to what has been acquired previously. Too frequently pupils are require to achieve concepts and generalizations which are too complex. Scaffolding may be utilized here in that the pupil is achieving at a selected level, but needs to attain more optimally. Thus, the social studies teacher assists the learner with brief explanations or questions which lead to the desired level of attainment (See Parker, 2001).

Fourth, creativity is a salient objective in that progress in society might well come from unique, original ideas secured by learners individually or within a committee setting. Thus, art, music, poetry, as well as other kinds of activities which inspire originality are important. An open-ended curriculum in which pupils feel the need to reveal novelty of ideas must be encouraged. Social studies subject matter might well provide the springboard for the creative mind (Ediger and Rao, 2011).

Fifth, problem solving is a must! In school and in society, learners face problems which need identification and viable solutions. Thus, within social studies lessons and units of study, pupils with teacher assistance need to utilize ongoing resources and materials of instruction to select relevant problem areas. The problem needs to be adequately delimited so that relevant answers/solutions may be found, resulting in a tentative hypothesis which is subject to evaluation with the use of appropriate information sources. The hypothesis might then be accepted, refuted, or revised. Thinking in depth is inherent here due to information sources needing to be assessed in terms of criteria.

Sixth, the room environment must be such that pupils are encouraged and have an inward desire to learn. Freedom from needless tension and within an atmosphere of respect must be emphasized. Rudeness and disrespect should have no role in ongoing lessons and units of study. Good citizenship must prevail in the school setting. Pupils with teacher guidance need to develop and enforce quality rules of conduct in the classroom. This is a very salient facet of social studies teaching.

REFERENCES

Ediger, Marlow and D. Bhaskara Rao (2007), *Teaching Social Studies.* New Delhi, India: Discovery Publishing House Ltd.

Ediger, Marlow and D. Bhaskara Rao (2011), *Essays in Teaching Social Studies.* New Delhi, India: Discovery Publishing House Ltd.

Parker, Walter C. (2001), *Social Studies in Elementary Education.* Upper Saddle River, New Jersey; Prentice-Hall, Inc.

Meeting Esteem Needs of Pupils in the Social Studies

Pupils need to attain as optimally as possible in the curriculum, social studies being no exception. Learners, presently, will be citizens of tomorrow and social studies learnings must make its many contributions. Thus, social studies teachers need to choose objectives with deliberation and thought, select appropriate learning opportunities to achieve these objectives, and emphasize evaluation procedures which are valid and reliable to appraise learner progress.

Holistic development of the learner is of utmost importance. The physical, emotional, social, and intellectual development of learners need integration into each unit of study.

Teaching and Learning in the Social Studies

A major objective in meeting esteem needs is to develop pupils' feelings of success in learning. Here, pupils interact with appropriate learning experiences and accomplish personal goals. Interest in learning assists pupils to put forth effort in achieving knowledge in history, geography, economics, political science and anthropology/sociology. The social studies teacher must be well acquainted with each pupil in terms of background knowledge and skills possessed before launching a new unit of study. He/she takes a personal interest in each learner and listens carefully to subject matter pupils present in ongoing discussions. It is good for the teacher to keep anecdotal records of pupils where dated entries are made to keep track of what pupils know and have left to learn. In this way, the social studies teacher may build upon previous learnings acquired by pupils. New objectives then to be acquired provide for improved sequence in ongoing learning activities. Success in learning builds confidence in the self with esteem needs being met (Ediger, 2007).

Second, pupils need to be rewarded for achievement in the curriculum. Verbal praise for quality progress made builds morale for learning. Pupils have an inward desire to feel a need for being rewarded for accomplishments. To go to school each day and feel that learning is not rewarded makes for a lack of motivation. Pupils individually as well as in committees must feel they are achieving well and this comes to fruition when a verbal reward is forthcoming.

Third, pupil interest is a powerful factor in achievement. Learning may be intrinsically motivating when there is a thirst for knowledge and skills in ongoing social studies units. When facts, concepts and generalizations become interesting to pupils, pupil motivation comes from within to accomplish, achieve, and grow. With interest in ongoing social studies units of study, pupils inwardly reach out for new knowledge and skills. The teacher's role here is to choose learning opportunities which capture and nurture. He/she needs to observe pupils if active active engagement in learning is forthcoming. Involvement in tasks, duties and responsibilities in each lesson taught should capture learner interests. The learner and the social studies become one and not separated from each other. Interest in learning propels pupils to put forth effort in attaining vital personal goals in the curriculum. Intrinsically with interest, esteem needs are being met with an inward desire for acquiring further knowledge and skills (See Parker, 2001).

Fourth, a quality classroom climate invites pupils to interact positively with others and with different materials of instruction. Cooperative endeavors, as a result, become satisfying as a means of goal attainment. A good learning atmosphere then emphasizes the following:

- respect and acceptance of others in the school setting
- feelings of caring and wanting to assist others, as needed
- positive attitudes with no leeway for rudeness, harassment, ill-will and retribution
- freedom to move around to secure needed materials and supplies as well as to interact with others
- acceptance of ideas expressed and not interrupting others when communicating content within a committee setting (Ediger, 2009).

With satisfying small group work, there is assistance for pupils in developing self esteem. Too frequently, learning opportunities are boring and fail to challenge the individual or group. With experiences which promote happiness in ongoing tasks, the pupil tends to feel good about the self and motivates achievement and learning.

Fifth, self efficacy is promoted with indepth acquisition of relevant subject matter. Improved preparation from rich past experiences helps pupils to tackle increasingly complex ideas in the social studies. Quality work in completing assignments and volunteering to complete additional activities should make the pupil increasingly proficient in the different academic branches of the social sciences. Integration of content here provides information for indepth problem solving in which there is a problem, hypothesis, and means of testing the hypothesis. Problem solving might well be emphasized as an enrichment a activity as well as within an ongoing unit of study. Self-efficacy or motivated efforts to achieve whereby the pupil feels confidence in learning is salient (See Ray, 2006).

Sixth, reflection upon previous experiences builds confidence in reviewing major concepts and generalizations in noticing their accuracy as well as completeness. If inaccuracies or incompleteness are noted through reflection, the pupil may pursue individual experiences to take care of deficiencies noted. A concern exists for wholeness in pursuing social studies knowledge and skills. Esteem needs are met in desiring correctness in the academics.

Seventh, purposeful learning experiences are important. If a pupil perceives purpose or reasons for learning, then reasons for making progress should abound. To frequently, assignments are made in the social studies with no accompanying reasons being provided for their completion. The learner needs to be motivated to perceive inherent reasons. He/she feels energized when perceived purpose is accepted by the pupil. If, for example, the pupil is a participant in a social studies fair, then a purpose will be to do well in completing a project and

- providing reasons for engaging in this experience.
- indicating plans for doing the project.
- stating the criteria for its evaluation.

A social studies fair where projects are judged in terms of quality as well as in daily work in the classroom, pupils can have esteem needs met. This is certainly a possibility for all pupils!

REFERENCES

Ediger, Marlow (2007), "Teacher Observation to Assess Student Achievement," *Journal of Instructional Psychology*, 34 (2), 137-139.

Ediger, Marlow (2009), "The Principal in the Teaching and Learning Process," *Education*, 129 (4), 574-578.

Parker, Walter C. (2001), *Social Studies in Elementary Education*, Upper Saddle River, New Jersey: Prentice-Hall, Inc.

Ray, Katie Wood (2006), "What Are You Thinking?", *Educational Leadership*, 64 (2), 58-62.

Data Driven Decision-making in the Social Studies

Data driven decision-making emphasizes the importance of the teacher using objective sources of information in developing the social studies curriculum. Too frequently, decisions of teachers have been made based on routine and outdated methods of teaching. Valid and reliable tests used to secure results from pupil learning make for better selection of objectives, learning opportunities and appraisal procedures. Pupils must make continuous progress in ongoing lessons and units of study in the social studies. Teacher use of data provides opportunities in making for quality pupil sequence in the social studies.

Securing Data

Tests used to evaluate pupil academic achievement must be valid in that they measure accurately in the respective academic discipline. Thus, a social studies test must measure pupil knowledge in this academic field. The test also needs to measure consistently so that the teacher has precise knowledge of what the pupil knows in the social studies. Reliability may consist of test/retest, alternative forms and/or split half reliability. The objectives for each test should be available to social studies teachers for use in teaching and learning situations. This makes for greater validity in teaching as compared to pupils being tested on unfamiliar subject matter.

Pupil standardized test results need to provide an overview of a learner's overall achievement as compared to others in the norm group upon which the test was standardized. Thus, percentile ranks, grade equivalent, and stanines are given in the Manual which may then be matched with each pupil's test results in the social studies. It must be realized that pupils differ from each other in a plethora of ways including abilities possessed, intelligence and motivation. Of utmost importance is to compare how well the pupil did as compared to previous test results. Each pupil should make optimal progress from one testing to the other. Teachers need to have test results pertaining to which test items were missed by the learner. He/she might then plan how each pupil may achieve more optimally in the social studies by basing instruction on test items missed.

The test item missed should have broad implications for teaching social studies, not narrow factual information. The broad implications include concepts, generalizations and main ideas. These may be tested in ensuing learning opportunities and are useful in many situations, in school and in society (Ediger, 2008).

Standardized tests are generally given once a year and comparisons for each pupil may be made in achievement from one year to the next. In the mean time, teacher written tests, properly Grafted, may provide valuable feedback on learner progress. These test should also be valid. The teacher of social studies may write a multiple choice test item as he/she teaches a concept, generalization and/or main idea. Face validity is then being stressed. It is not good to ask test questions for which pupils have had little/no previous opportunity for learning. These test items lack validity. In writing each multiple choice test item, the social studies teacher needs to:

- write a stem (not all have stems) which harmonizes grammatically with four distractors.
- write distractors which are all plausible. The following is not a plausible distractor: The first president of the United States was (a) Mickey Mouse.
- write distractors of similar length so as not to provide clues as to which is the correct (or incorrect) answer.

- provide no clues in writing as to which is the correct response such as: The capitol cities of Saudi Arabia are (*a*) Riyad and Mecca, (*b*) Ammon, (*c*) Damascus, (*d*) Baghdad.

By developing high quality tests, the teacher has a much better opportunity of obtaining relevant data for social studies curricular decision making. If test items are poorly written, the teacher has little to go by in improving social studies instruction (Ediger, 2008).

True/false test items have merit in evaluating pupils achievement if they attempt to eliminate the possibility of excessive guessing, otherwise the pupil has a fifty percent chance of guessing correct responses. Notice the following true/false test item: The Sea of Galilee is the largest body of water in the land of Palestine. The answer is false. The pupil needs to change what is false to make the previous statement true. Thus, *The Dead Sea* is the largest body of water in the land of Palestine.

Matching test items in the social studies, carefully written by the teacher, provide information from test results for teaching and learning situations. Multiple choice test items need to follow the following criteria:

- there should be more items in one column than the other in order to minimize the process of elimination to come up with correct answers. It is always good to match known items in column A with the correct response in column B first, then the remainder has a few extra items to avoid guessing which is correct. The teacher desires to have accurate, relevant information from test results in order to improve sequence and accuracy of knowledge.
- one of the two columns should have words or short phrases only, not complete sentences. It becomes exceedingly complex if both columns for matching have complete sentences.
- the written matching test should harmonize with the developmental level of the test taker. Thus, the test

may be too lengthy or too short depending upon the mental maturity level of the pupil. Words used must be on the understanding level of test takers (See Burke 2005).

Essay tests written by the teacher provide opportunities for pupils to organizing ideas, sequence written content, as well as indicate breadth and depth in learning. Clarity of ideas expressed is of utmost importance which must be meaningful to the reader of the essay test items. The pupil, here, is attempting to communicate content in writing. If long hand is used, then quality handwriting needs to be emphasized. Additional mechanics in written work include proper punctuation, grammar, letter formation, capitalization of words, and as well as alignment of letters and words. Essay test items need to adhere to the following standards:

- be on the developmental level of the involved learners
- be valid and aligned with the objectives of the lesson/ unit of study
- be meaningfully written so that pupils know what is wanted in terms of responses
- be written so that creative and critical thinking, as well as problem solving are stressed
- be evaluated with quality rubric assistance. Rubric results can emphasize interscorer reliability if several evaluate the same essays using the criteria in the rubric (Ediger, 2007).

With teacher written tests, pupils have opportunities to reveal intrinsically what has been accomplished and the resulting information may be highly useful to pinpoint specifics in what is left to learn. These test items truly reflect what is taught in a unit of study.

They may not possess the validity and reliability inherent in pilot studied and analyzed standardized tests, also called norm referenced tests distinguishable from criterion referenced tests.

To improve unit teaching in the social studies, the teacher must secure vital test information from pupils. *Formative* evaluation stresses the importance of securing information of pupil learning along the way when the unit is implemented. This gives chances for the teacher to make revisions and modifications before the unit ends. Thus, from feedback obtained, the teacher may make necessary changes in objectives to be emphasized in teaching, learning activities to achieve these objectives, as well as the appraisal procedures themselves.

Summative evaluation emphasizes end of unit appraisal. When the social studies unit has been completed, the teacher views test results from summative evaluation. Here, in reviewing the data, the social studies teacher attempts to answer the following:

- which changes should be made in the unit of study for the next school year?
- what modifications need to be made in the objectives, the learning opportunities, as well as the appraisal procedures?
- which grouping procedures, if any, in the classroom should be changed?
- how much stress needs to be placed upon individual versus cooperative endeavors in learning?
- should enrichment activities be included as motivators for learning? (See National Council for the Social Studies, 2008).

There are schools and teachers who emphasize benchmarks in achievement. Thus, there are goals which learners need to achieve within a unit at an approximate time. The social studies teacher may then evaluate what pupils have accomplished and what is left to learn. This is a time for reflection and further planning to optimize learner achievement.

There are cautions to observe in testing pupils. These include the following:

- pupils may be tested too frequently, especially when other methods of appraisal are useful such as teacher observation of pupil achievement. Adequate time must be available for instruction, also.

- pupils may refrain from putting forth effort in test taking if too many are given.
- there are a plethora of additional methods to determine what pupils have learned, than standardized and other forms of paper/pencil tests
- pupil fatigue may set in with too many tests to taken.

There are plethora of additional methods to use in appraising learner achievement, than testing. These include the following in the social studies:

- teacher observation, briefly referred to above. Here, the social studies teacher may notice immediately where a pupil needs more assistance. Thus, a pupil may need help with understanding and drawing lines of latitude and longitude in geography.
- discussion settings in which learners reveal they do not attach meaning to the concepts of time in history as in the French Revolution related to other events in context. Assistance might well then be provided for pupils to develop greater insights into this period of time.
- a debate involving governmental intervention versus the free enterprise system in health care provisions, in the political science and economics domain.
- a chart developed within a committee to show the influence of culture on human behavior (See Ahmad, 2009).

Somewhat opposite of measurement psychology of instruction is constructivism. Constructivism emphasizes the following:

- a pupil centered approach in teaching whereby they are actively involved in the instructional arena
- pupil/teacher planning of objectives, learning activities, and evaluation procedures
- pupils sequence their own individual learnings

- pupils with teacher guidance learn by discovery methods
- testing is greatly minimized. Teacher observation and pupil self evaluation are used in assessment.

REFERENCES

Ahmad, Sajjad (2009), "Evolving A Framework for Teaching and Learning," *Edutracks*, 8 (9), 11-12. Published in India.

Burke, Karen (2005), "Teacher Certification Exams: What are the Predictors of Success?" *College Student Journal*, 39 (4), 784-793.

Ediger, Marlow (2007), "Teacher Observation to Assess Student Achievement," *Journal of Instructional Psychology*, 34 (3), 137-139.

Ediger, Marlow (2008), "Leadership in the School Setting," *Education*, 129 (1), 17-20.

Ediger, Marlow (2008), "The School and Students in Society," *Journal of Instructional Psychology*, 35 (3), 260-263.

National Council for the Social Studies (2008), "A Vision of Powerful Teaching and Learning in the Social Studies: Building Effective Citizens," *Social Education*, 72 (5), 277-280.

Rating Teachers of Social Studies Instruction

Teachers are being increasingly held accountable for their quality of student instruction. They need to prepare well for each lesson taught and provide for individual differences among learners. Documentation of teaching success is desired. Tracking results of teacher effectiveness is salient. Thus, there needs to be an effective approach to use in noticing how well each teacher is doing in time.

Quality of Criteria in Rating

Standards used in the rating process must be carefully chosen with heavy involvement of teachers, supervisors and school administrators. They need careful research, scrutiny and study, prior to implementation. Social studies is a highly important academic discipline and needs to be included in any mandated system of testing to indicate its saliency. There are a plethora of reasons to be given for the importance of the social studies. A major reason being that threats to humanity exist if nations continually spend excessive amount of money on the military as well as plan attacks against each other. Deaths, destruction, and wounded individuals result. Post-traumatic stress is commonly discussed and this involves traumas veterans experience from actual fighting in wars. Ways need to be found to minimize/eliminate militaristic fervor among inhabitants of any nation.

There are a plethora of ways to spend moneys to benefit humanity such as quality, affordable health care. Too may people go bankrupt when a costly malady hits a family. Then to moneys may be spent on improving infrastructure of an area such as safe roads, bridges, flood control projects and safety in cities. Crime is rampant in certain areas where hostile gangs operate. More police and fire protection is necessary, the latter is indicated with the many cases of arson occurring.

Corruption in corporations is very costly to society with extremely high salaries paid to CEOs and board members, even with a failing economic operation. In addition stock options, and bonuses add to these unfortunate ventures. Morality and ethics are certainly a problem and a major one at that.

Thus, there are numerous reasons which might well be given to stressing strong social studies curricula in the public schools. This must include economic development, a democratic society, achievements in medical science, accomplishments in the fine arts and in architecture, as well as high productivity in agriculture, among others. Social studies teachers must provide leadership to emphasize quality in the curriculum. Quality may come from well prepared teachers, continual inservice education, adequate and purposeful teaching materials of instruction, support from school administrators and curriculum directors and cooperating parents (Ediger, 2009). The question then arises,"How should social studies teachers be appraised?"

First, social studies teachers must become efficacious in that they are highly knowledgeable and confident in their chosen profession. They possess not only the knowledge but also needed methodology to provide for individual differences among pupils. Pupils are the focal point of attention. They must do the learning and be assisted to attain optimally in the social studies. Thus, pupils need to achieve well in subject matter, in skills, and in attitudes (Ediger, 2008).

Second, developing good citizens should be at the heart of teaching and learning situations. The social studies teacher needs to serve as a model. He/she needs to take an active role in societal responsibilities, exemplify good human relations, manage personal finances effectively, and develop a good self concept. The social studies teacher guides pupils to be very knowledgeable about being/implementing standards of being a good citizen. This is more than passing tests, which is important, but also there needs to be the desire to improve society for the benefit of all (See Smith and Lambert, 2008).

Third, achieving advanced university degrees in the social sciences assists in developing leadership qualities to improve in the teaching of the social studies. The social studies teacher must experience quality course work in history, geography, economics, political science, anthropology/sociology, and psychology. What is studied on the university level needs to become a salient part of instruction in the public school setting. Teacher preparation programs in schools of education then should not be separated from actual public school teaching/learning situations. Connections must be made (See Petress, 2006).

Fourth, lesson and unit construction must be designed to meet cognitive, affective and psychomotor needs of pupils. Incorporated in each must stress the following psychological principles of learning:

- engagement of each learner in ongoing learning activities
- purposeful experiences whereby pupils perceive reasons for achieving
- provisions made for multiple intelligences in the classroom as well as styles of learning
- meaning and understanding emphasized
- challenge and success for learners inherent in planning for instruction (See Phillips, 2008).

By integrating the above named principles of learning in ongoing instruction, pupils should achieve more optimally in the social studies.

Fifth, classroom standards of conduct should be developed cooperatively involving the social studies teacher and learners. Reasons for these standards are to enhance learning and not for the sake of their development. The classroom environment should be such that pupils can achieve objectives in a satisfactory manner. This means that the classroom environment:

- stresses a business like atmosphere for learning
- politeness for all is in evidence. This must be true for teachers as well as pupils.

Sixth, acceptance of others is vital regardless of cultural backgrounds including religion, nationality, languages spoken, and native customs, among others. Too frequently, pupils are shunned who come from a primary group or another nation. If all are to attain more optimally, they need to develop feelings of belonging. Democracy as a way of life indicates that all are equal before the law and therefore each person needs to possess feelings of equality of opportunity in human relations as well as in classroom endeavors. Learning opportunities need to emphasize this importance when provisions are made for individual differences in the classroom. Pupils come to the classroom with different interests, talents, and hobbies. Feelings of acceptance occur when esteem needs are met of learners. Pupils individually may not be rewarded for contributions made. Thus, esteem needs fail to be met of pupils, individually. All have something valuable to contribute including English Language Learners (ELL), slow learners, as well as those who are mainstreamed.

Seventh, integrated subject matter from the academic disciplines must be emphasized. In any social studies unit of study, the teacher may plan to integrate content to assist pupils to achieve well and to see connectedness. Content perceived as being related will be remembered longer than if perceived as isolated facts. For example, the following unit of study on Japan in terms of each academic discipline indicates the possibility of perceived relationships:

- the history of relevant concepts and generalizations to be stressed

- geographical features comprising islands which makeup the nation of Japan
- economic development which has aided Japan in becoming a leading industrial nation
- the system and organization of government (political science)
- the music, art, architecture, foods eaten, music, level of technology, and culture of Japan

The social studies teacher needs to relate academic disciplines where it is feasible and good to do so. The curriculum must be adapted to the present achievement levels of pupils. Continuous progress of learners is then achieved sequentially. Indepth teaching is recommended of major concepts and generalizations. A variety of materials of instruction must be used to capture and maintain pupil interest such as:

- concrete objects including models and objects of Japan
- semi-concrete materials including video tapes, power point presentations, illustrations and pictures,
- abstract print materials such as basal textbooks, library books, resource personnel, as well as computerized programs (See Balathy, 2007).

In Closing

Criteria were discussed pertaining to appraising social studies teachers. These are flexible criteria and may be written more concisely to use in ratings given by responsible persons (students, teachers and school administrators) to social studies teachers. Feedback needs to be given to assist in developing quality teachers of the social studies.

REFERENCES

Balathy, Ernest (2007), "Technology and Current Reading/Literacy Assessment Strategies," *Reading Teacher*, 61 (3), 240-248.

Ediger, Marlow (2008), "Current Events in the Social Studies," *Social Studies Review*, 47 (2), 58-60.

Ediger, Marlow (2009) "Scope in the Social Studies," *Edutracks*, 8 (6), 14-16.

Petress, Ken (2006), "An Operational Definition of Class Participation," *College Student Journal*, 40 (4), 821-823.

Phillips, Antoinette, *et al.*, (2008), "Enhancing a Curriculum: A Focus on the Developmental Process," *College Student Journal*, 42 (4), 1070-1074.

Smith, Rick, and Mary Lambert (2008), "Assuming the Best," *Educational Leadership*, 66 (1), 16-21.

Chapter 23 Assisting English Language Learners in an Integrated Class in the Social Studies

With a plethora of children speaking another language than English in the school setting, it behooves the teacher to possess a repertoire of teaching skills which promote proficiency in English language usage. English language learners (ELL) need to become effective in language use in school and in society so they may become productive societal members. At the same time, their native language must be respected. Ridicule, rudeness and minimizing those of another language definitely must be prohibited. Rather, an atmosphere of respect needs to prevail toward all in the classroom and school setting. Acceptance of others assists, too, in learning about other cultures. This aids in providing for a rich learning environment when pupils can learn from each others' cultures and customs. ELL students might well be taught in an integrated classroom with other children in the regular classroom. The examples provided pertain to a unit of study in the social studies and the model presented may apply to all classrooms. Additional experiences, carefully chosen, aid in achieving relevant objectives in each unit of study. Jerome Bruner stated that, "Any subject matter can be learned by any child in any stage of development in some intellectually, honest form." This manuscript is based on that principle.

Learning Activities Designed in an Integrated Curriculum

Concrete experiences must be emphasized frequently for ELL and all pupils. Thus, for example, in a unit on the Middle East with emphasis on the West and East Bank of the Jordan River, the teacher may present objects from an interest centre, pertaining to this region of the world (Ediger and Rao, 2011):

- olive wood carved items such as a model of the Dome of the Rock, a beautiful octagonal Muslim mosque with a gold plated dome, located on Mount Moriah inside the walled city of Jerusalem; a model of the Western Wall, the only remnant of the ancient Jewish Temple, located directly west of the Dome of the Rock and a model of the Church of the Holy Sepulcher, which houses the Tomb of Christ and is also located inside the walled city.
- a mother of pearl model showing the Last Supper with Christ and his twelve apostles; a model seven stick Menorah which signified the Jews taking back the Temple by the Macabees from Syrian rule in 67 BC; and a copy of the Koran, the holy book of the Muslims.

The social studies teacher needs to hold up each object when teaching so pupils can observe them carefully. Thus, in sequence, the teacher may hold up the model of the Dome of the Rock for all to focus upon in the classroom. Sentences spoken must be clear and brief with the teacher pointing to each part of this structure as it is being presented. The eight sides (geometrically octagonal) need clarification in that it supports the dome part of the building. This mosque is a place of worship for devout Muslims.

A comparison might then be made with the model of the Western Wall, also held up by the teacher when teaching and visible to all. The huge stones in the Wall, as is true of all learning experiences, need clarification as to their meaning in being a place of worship. This is the last remnant of the ancient Jewish Temple. Jewish worshipers gather here each day for services. The third model, the Church of the Holy Sepulcher, may be contrasted with the two previous models as being holy to devout Christians in housing the Tomb of Christ.

A time line with accompanying illustrations may show the sequence of building the three structures. The Dome of the Rock in AD 691, the ancient Jewish Temple approximately 1000 BC, and the present church of the Holy Sepulcher in AD 1099. The time line extends meanings of the three structures in terms of three religions born in the Middle East. Enlarged textbook content shown on a screen which comes from internet sources needs to be read collectively by pupils with teacher guidance. Related electronic illustrations shown and discussed help learners to understand the above named three structures. Thus, a variety of learning opportunities assists in providing for each pupil in the classroom as well as enriching the social studies curriculum.

The Last Supper Model, the Menorah, and the Koran provide rich experiences for learners in terms of the historical and geographical birth place of three religions in the Middle East; the land of Palestine for Judaism and Christianity, and Islam (Muslim) in what is now Saudi Arabia. These places need location on a map and on a globe. Additional map/globe exercises need implementation, including making/drawing a map of the Middle East with an attached legend.

A Framework for Indepth Unit Teaching

Structural ideas will now be discussed in terms of major ideas for the teacher, inductively/deductively, to present as well as for learner acquisition. Judaism had its beginning when the Patriarch Abraham was called out of Ur of the Ghaldees (now Iraq) to the land of Palestine, in 1800 BC. His son Isaac and grandson Jacob, in succession, carried out the habitation in Palestine. The latter and his family moved to Egypt due to a severe famine. Jacob's son Joseph who had been sold into slavery, forty years earlier, had become second in command to Pharaoh. His task was to gather enough grain for human and livestock use, during the years of plenty to take care of the drouth years when none was produced. After leaving Egypt under duress, the Israelites with Moses as the leader wandered for forty years in the Sinai peninsula and then entered Palestine. In the Sinai, the Ten Commandments were secured on two stone tablets by Moses. His successor, Joshua, lead the Israelites into Palestine. This land was divided into tribal territories, each tribe basically was represented by the twelve sons of Jacob, such as his son Rueben receiving a tract of land in Palestine, among the other sons. In 1000 BC, King David ruled for forty years. His successor and son, King Solomon built the ancient Jewish Temple and extended the nation in size, from the Nile to the Euphrates. Further key ideas include the following:

- the Babylonian captivity of Jews beginning in 587 BC until selected exiles returned to Palestine, approximately fifty years later.
- the rule of the Maccabean Jews, 167-66 BC, Roman Empire rule, 100 BC to the beginning of the Byzantine Empire and Constantine the Great AD 330; and The Ottoman Empire rule from 1517-1917. These may all be emphasized with videos covering each period of time. There are numerous companies which have these which include realistic settings for dress, appearance, housing, means of transportation, shopping places, roads and paths, foods eaten and places for livestock and crops grown, among others. Meaning, interest, and understanding are to be stressed, not rote learning. A carefully designed social studies unit with appropriate scope and sequence are to be included. Dates, listed above, might be shown by assisting learners to view a time line with a digital illustration for each.
- Great Britain received the League of Nations Mandate in 1917 with the incorporation of the Balfour Declaration providing for a Jewish Homeland in Palestine; many Jews left Nazi Germany during World War II due to persecution, imprisonment in concentration camps, as well as extreme discrimination. This mass migration lead to the establishment of the state of Israel in 80 per cent of the land of Palestine.
- in 1967, Israel captured the rest of Palestine (20%) from the nation of Jordan and 500,000 Jewish settlers moved to and now live in what was formerly the West Bank of the Jordan.

The above key ideas, look at the other side of the equation. These many wars have been very costly to the Arabs in Palestine. There were approximately 700,000 Arab refugees from the 1948 War. The writer served on the West Bank as a teacher at Friends Boys School at Ramallah and assisted in clothing distributions in Palestinian Arab Refugee camps, Aqaba Jabber and Einsultan camps near Jericho, in the early 1950s. These two years were served in lieu of military service.

Mohammed, the last prophet, according to devout Muslims, was born in AD 570 in Mecca in what is one of two capitol cities in Saudi Arabia. There were a plethora of deities worshiped in Mecca at that time. There was one deity for each day of the year. Mohammed married a wealthy widow and managed her caravans as they travelled to distant places for business purposes. He learned about Jewish and Christian religious beliefs in his travels. Later, Mohammed had time for meditation, which he engaged in frequently. He had thoughts and visions and these he recorded with the help of the angel Gabriel. Followers adopted his religious beliefs and forsook the worshiping of the original deities surrounding Mecca. As the number of followers increased in number, there was outrage by those making and monitoring the human deities. Their business and profits shrunk in the offing. Ultimately, Mohammed and has followers fled Mecca for safety reasons, going 200 miles north to Medina. At Medina, the followers of Mohammed greatly increased in number and they returned to and overtook Mecca. A century later, Muslims, having greatly increased in population, captured the walled city of Jerusalem and their power extended to taking over much of France in Western Europe when the Muslims were finally defeated at the Battle of Poiters. In 1099, The Crusaders captured Jerusalem from the Muslims in what became known a the Crusades, a series of wars to wrest the Holy Land by the Crusaders from Muslim rule. Eventually in the thirteenth century, Muslim rule prevailed.

Mohammed (570-632) and his followers established what became known as the five Pillars of Islam. The first being the

Creed, "There is no God but Allah and Mohammed is His prophet." The Creed is said in Arabic and Allah means God. Their Holy Book is the *Koran,* also written in Arabic, but has been translated into other languages. A second pillar of Islamic faith is praying at designated times, five times a day facing Mecca, their holiest city and birth place of Mohammed. Our gatekeeper at the Mennonite Central Committee (MCC) center in Jericho, Hajj, was a very devout Muslim. He faithfully said his prayers early in the morning when a thread cannot be distinguished between being white our black. His prayers were very clear and distinct, according to the general ritual of Muslims. Nothing distracted his prayers while facing Mecca. He was asked one day what he would do if there was a fire in a building on the MCC grounds while praying. His answer was that the prayer must first be finished regardless of the consequences.

A third pillar of Islam is to give annually two and one half per cent of one's total worth to needy people. This was called giving of alms. In 1952-1954, approximately fifty per cent of the Arab population were unemployed and many were refugees of the first Arab/Israeli War of 1948. About 700,000 Arab refugees were the result with two large camps—Aqaba Jabber to the south side and Einsulten to the north Jericho, among other camps. Early in the morning, refugees would come from these two camps to obtain water from Elisha's Fountain in Jericho, named after an Old Testament prophet. This fountain is a spring of which there are many in the Holy Land. It was a colorful, yet depressing scene of women carrying water jugs on their heads as well as an infant from the spring to the refugee camps.

A fourth pillar of Islam is to make an annual trip, if health and age permit, to their holy city of Mecca. Among other things, pilgrims drink water from the well Zem Zem, which devout Muslims believe Hagar the maiden of Abraham, saw after fleeing with her son Ishmael, son of Abraham. Also, the Kaaba, located near to the well Zem Zem, is encircled seven times. The Kaaba was built by the Patriarch Abraham and his son Ishmael, according to Muslim faith.

A fifth pillar stresses fasting during the holiest month of the year which is Ramadan. The fasting is done from sunrise to sunset. There are a few exceptions here, such as aged individual and ill persons.

The Christian religion has numerous salient happenings in their history. According to Christianity, Jesus was born in Bethlehem, six miles south of Jerusalem. This city has the Church of the Nativity containing the grotto area and crypt of his birth. Tourists flock to Bethlehem at all times of the year and especially at Christmas time. Thirteen miles south is the city of Hebron, containing the Tomb of the Prophets, also called the Mosque of Abraham. Inside this building are the tombs of the Patriarch Abraham and his wife Sarah, his son Isaac and wife Rebecca, as well as Jacob, the grandson and his wife Leah. Ninety miles north of Jerusalem is the city of Nazareth where the Church of the Annunciation is located. Here the announcement of the oncoming birth of Jesus was made to his mother Mary, according to devout followers of Christianity. On the Mount of Olives, directly east of the walled city of Jerusalem, are a plethora of Churches which attempted to pinpoint specific places where important happenings of Christianity occurred:

- the Garden of Gethsemanee, a meeting place for Jesus and his twelve disciplines.
- the Russian Orthodox church of the Ascension which has a spire pointing heavenward.
- The Russian Orthodox Church, with onion shaped domes, also a place commemorating the Garden of Gethsemanee.

When serving as MCC relief worker and teacher, 1952-1954, on the West Bank which consisted of twenty per cent of the land of Palestine was made up largely of Muslims with fifteen percent being Christian in religion. At that time, there were none of the Jewish faith on the West Bank. The walled city of Jerusalem was entirely in the West Bank (the geographical areas can be shown largely on a wall map). Around the wall, the distance is two and one half miles and has eight entrances or gates. The Damascus gate is on the north side and leads inside to the busiest shopping areas. These are generally small stalls with entrances from the narrow winding street. For example, one small stall may have gunny sacks filed with almonds, pecans, walnuts, or other small grains as well as with figs or dates. The small grains are utilized to flavor rice dishes. For clothing sales, the western style or bedouin clothes are hung on a hangar, against the wall. Souvenir shops abound with models of items salient to the three different faiths of Judaism, Islam and Christianity.

Conclusion

The described unit brings to the attention of pupils, not only religious beliefs, as well as their differences among the three faiths, but also the following:

- strong disagreements as to who owns and governs which territories and areas in the land of Palestine.
- the issue of return of captured/occupied land in the 1967 Arab-Israeli war.
- building of settlements in land gained from war.
- the role major world powers play in the Holy Land area.

REFERENCE

Ediger, Marlow and D. Bhaskara Rao (2011), *Essays on Teaching Social Studies*. New Delhi, India: Discovery Publishing House Ltd. The first named author was a relief worker and teacher, 1952-1954, with the Mennonite Central Committee (MCC), making five return trips to this area of the world.

Enjoyment in the Mathematics Curriculum

Wholesome attitudes are salient to develop in any curriculum area, mathematics being no exception. Many pupils like mathematics; others may not develop this quality attitude. The attitudinal dimension is salient to develop in school and in society. Higher accomplishments are then possible. With good attitudes, achievement in mathematics can be optimized.

Too frequently, mathematics may become routine and drudgery. This certainly need not be so. A motivated teacher may select and irnplement those activities which provide enjoyment at the same time objectives of instruction are being acquired. Enjoyment and achievement of objectives need not be separated from each other, but can well become integrated entities (Ediger, 2006).

The Affective Dimension in Teaching and Learning

The pupil is the focal point of instruction. He/she needs to perceive mathematics as being positive, useful and good. The learner experiences and reaches conclusions. Hopefully, the learner will develop positive feelings of wanting to learn more mathematical content and skills. These inward feelings should result. The teacher designs and implements what was planned for teaching and learning experiences. The interest factor must be thoroughly considered with the following in mind:

- providing a variety of activities such as those requiring a hands on approach with real objects in doing the four basic operations of addition, subtraction, multiplication, and division.

- emphasis also being placed upon visual representations of reality including pictorial forms, computerized programs with illustrations, video tape and power point slides, showing, for example, geometrical figures, plane and solid geometry, as well as calculations involving reasoning and problem solving. The writer when supervising university student teachers in the public schools observed an interesting lesson on geometry art for young children. The supervising teacher and the student teacher cut geometrical figures from different colours of construction paper. Pupils selected geometrical figures to portray people, buildings, among other items, on drawing paper. The products were posted on the bulletin board for viewing. Pupils had to name each figure as being a circle, square, triangle, rhombus, etc. Pupils from other classrooms came in to observe and comment on the geometry art project. Enthusiasm and interest were high.
- abstractions which indicate how the real and the pictorial may be represented numerically and used in school/society. For example, a picture graph was developed by pupils showing a photo of each in the month of birth. Other picture graphs were shown and discussed; pupils developed an understanding of why graphs are used to present data (See Kennedy and Tipps, 1991).

Interest factors involve wholehearted involvement by learners. Well planned lessons with appropriate use of teaching aids assist pupils in enjoying mathematics. The mathematics teacher's modulated voice with proper stress of words, pitch within sentences and juncture (pauses) attract learner attention to achieve objectives of instruction. Gestures should be positive and harmonize with deeds. The following personality traits need to be in the offing:

- politeness and respect

- caring and helpfulness
- positive attitudes toward teaching and learning
- feelings of excitement toward mathematics
- wanting to learn more about mathematical content
- willingness to work harmoniously with parents (See Brady, 2008).

If the teacher sequences learning opportunities, he/she must take care to have it be developmentally appropriate. If a pupil does not understand a mathematical process due to its difficulty, it might well hinder positive affective development whereas if it is too easy, then boredom might well set in. The mathematics teacher then has a problem in selecting learning opportunities which are developmentally appropriate. A pupil may attain a somewhat difficult learning through scaffolding whereby the teacher builds upon pupil knowledge possessed and then assists the learner to achieve the more complex mathematical understanding using cues, techniques, and experiences which help the pupil to achieve what formerly was too complex. Each step of learning, however, must be challenging and learner centered. The interests of pupils might well be cultivated through a challenging mathematical curriculum (See Cuban, 2008).

Adequate time, too, must be given to help pupils reflect upon what was learned. Metacognition emphasizes concepts pertaining to "thinking about thinking." Thus, the pupil needs assistance to reflect upon past mathematical experiences. The teacher might demonstrate aloud how metacognition operates to retain and strengthen understandings acquired. What is not understood is brought to the forefront and provides opportunities for meaningful clarification and reteaching. With meaning attached to ongoing teaching and learning experiences, pupils understand subject matter taught. Pupils are then ready to build new facts, concepts and generalizations based on previously understood content. Mastery of mathematical algorithms provides readiness to achieve new objectives of instruction. Indepth learning aids the pupil to understand, grow, accomplish and achieve. Interest, too, is furthered with the pupil truly attaching meaning to subsequent learnings (Ediger, 2008).

Self-efficacy is enhanced when teachers become increasingly knowledgeable of subject matter and skills. Confidence is then developed in the self. The mathematics teacher secures feelings of being able to teach and provide for pupils of different categories such as the gifted, English Language Learners (ELL), slow learners and the mentally retarded. There is this feeling of being successful in teaching a variety of kinds of pupils. Each pupil needs to attain as optimally as possible.

To possess feelings of enjoyment, pupils, too, need to feel that purpose is involved in learning. Reasons are then accepted for achieving salient objectives of instruction. How might the mathematics teacher assist pupils to perceive purpose in learning?

- to indicate relevancy in an ongoing lesson. For example, when pupils are studying how to determine area, they need help to see practical uses which can be made of the concept. Memorization, alone, does not guide pupils to perceive purpose. They need to understand each sequential step of learning, as well as perceive uses which can be made in school and in society. Uses to be made in finding the area include measuring classroom size, length and width, to notice the size of carpet which needs to be installed. The number of square feet, for example, may be meaningfully made by marking off squares, one foot by one foot, in the classroom. Pupils may then count the number of squares. The number of counted squares may be compared with taking the length of squares times the width of the squares which then equals the area of the classroom. Concrete and life like experiences assist pupils to use numerical values to represent reality. Sequential learning and practicality are two concepts which provide readiness for future accomplishments. The teacher must observe to notice that each sequence is meaningful and understood, resulting in the ultimate purpose of the learning, to determine the area of square feet in the classroom.

- to encourage the use of games to interest learners in mathematics. Computerize games are intriguing to many pupils if they are developmentally appropriate. The writer when supervising university student teachers has observed many pupils playing math games via the computer. Intrinsically, these are motivating to learners. Pupils respond to a problem on the monitor and then receive immediate feedback as to it correctness. Independently, the pupil may move forward sequentially on one or more games. Wholesome competition might also be brought in between opposing sides in attempting to be a winner. Computer programs may be used, also, as simulation, tutorial, drill and practice, and diagnostic/remediation. They need to be integrated into the regular mathematics curriculum (Ediger, 2009).

Pupils, too, have been fascinated with teacher made mathematics games. Here, the games are, ideally, aligned with the objectives in an ongoing unit of study. Order and sequence are built into each game, with enjoyment being a leading goal. Games assist pupils to review and rehearse previously acquired learnings. Active involvement of learners in gaming as well as in all learning activities is salient!

What to Avoid

Enjoyment, among others, must be a major goal for pupils to achieve in mathematics learning. Thus, there need to be pitfalls to avoid in the curriculum. The pitfalls include the following:

- criticism of pupils. Rather, what pupils do not understand should be clarified and appropriate learning activities used to remedy deficiencies.
- impatience. Too frequently, too much ground is being covered from basal textbooks in order to complete activities in a hurry, resulting in shallow learnings.

Instead, a quality indepth sequence needs to be in the offing so that new subject matter taught is based on previously well understood facts, concepts, and generalizations.

- rudeness and rude comments. If pupils do not attain as well as desired, the teacher must not ridicule learners but needs to examine his/her own procedures of instruction. A variety of learning opportunities must be used to assist pupils to achieve, grow and develop. Remedying deficiencies is needed to correct inaccurate learnings of pupils. This must be followed by using a developmental strategy of instruction.

REFERENCES

Brady, Marion (2008), "Cover the Material—Or Teach Children to Think", 65, (5), 64-67.

Cuban, Larry (2008), "The Perennial Reform: Fixing School Time," *Phi Delta Kappan*, 90 (4), 240-250.

Ediger, Marlow (2006), "Writing in the Mathematics Curriculum," *Journal of Instructional Psychology*, 33 (1), 120-123.

Ediger, Marlow (2008), "Modern School Mathematics," *The College Student Journal*, 42 (4), 986-989.

Ediger, Marlow (2009), "The Principal in the Teaching and Learning Process," *Education*, 129 (4), 574-578.

Kennedy, Leonard M. and Steve Tipps (1991), *Guiding Children's Learning of Mathematics*. Belmont, California: Wadsworth Publishing Company.

What Makes for a High Quality Mathematics Curriculum?

There are a plethora of recommendations as to the development of an optimal, relevant mathematics curriculum. There are selected goals which are recommended by national and state study groups. The National Council Teachers of Mathematics (NCTM), Common Core State Standards (CCSS) and No Child Left Behind (NCLB), among others. All agree that mathematics teachers must possess a solid core of vital subject matter to be used in instructional procedures. Mathematics teachers might then feel more secure in teaching and learning situations. Thus, they possess needed content to diagnose and remediate pupil difficulties in ongoing lessons as well as teach developmentally appropriate lessons. It takes knowledgeable and skilful teachers to ascertain what is needed in these situations. This means that mathematical knowledge alone is not adequate, but procedures and processes of instruction are also salient. Students need to be able to utilize necessary content within a specific situation. Practical as well as theoretical knowledge is salient and vital. There are a variety of specific situations whereby pupils individually and collectively need assistance and this requires the mathematics teacher to be creative in finding ways of assisting learners to be successful in mathematical usage (Ediger and Rao, 2011).

Recommendations for a High Quality Mathematics Curriculum

Mathematics teachers need to follow selected criteria to develop self efficacy in teaching and learning situations.

Emphasizing the ensuing will guide teachers to become proficient in working with pupils.

- collaborative endeavors are significant for learners. Thus within school and society, pupils need to harmonize ideas with those provided by others in a small group setting. Psychologist Len Vygotsky (1978), who is quoted widely in committee work, advocates strongly that learning is social and occurs within a group whereby subject matter is shared as in problem solving. Thus, ideas bounce off the minds of individuals and are modified when doing so in coming up with solutions in mathematical problem solving. Each pupil contributes in finding answers in the sharing session.
- individual work is also salient. This might well be preferable to those individuals who achieve best when working by the self in ongoing lessons and units of study. Pupils, here, possess initiative and motivation which propels learners to attain and progress. The emphasis is upon achievement for those learners who are motivated from within when pursuing ongoing activities. Perhaps, balance between cooperative and individual endeavor is the better approach since in society, persons work collectively as well as individually on projects, in leisure time experiences, as well as at the work place (Ediger, 2008).
- heterogeneous as well as homogeneous grouping should be emphasized in the mathematics classroom. There are times when the teacher needs to utilize the latter when teaching a specific process such as the commutative property of addition. These pupils need additional time to master the ensuing learnings. Thus, there are reasons for stressing a selected procedure of grouping pupils for instruction. At other times, a new lesson might stress mathematical subject matter whereby all in a classroom can benefit from the same/similar content being presented. The approach used in grouping for instruction chosen must assist optimal

learning, not grouping for the sake of grouping. Heterogeneous grouping might then be implemented. In society people interact with those of all capacity as well as ability levels.

- continuous evaluation of pupil progress must be in the offing. For example, a personal diary may be kept by the teacher, dating each entry, pertaining to a pupil's difficulties/errors in an ensuing mathematical lesson. Thus, continuous teacher observation of individual pupil's achievement must be in the offing to notice where assistance must be provided. Diagnosis and remediation are salient concepts to stress in mathematical achievement. Feedback, here, provides important ensuing learning activities which then might make for sequential pupil progress.
- inservice education should be stressed as being ongoing. Thus, workshops, faculty meetings, grade level or academic area seminars and reading professional literature on mathematics teaching, assists the teacher to develop to develop proficiency in the instructional arena. Additional areas of inservice growth include attending local, state and national conventions on mathematics teaching. Working toward an advanced degree in mathematics education from an accredited college/university must be considered carefully as a means of acquiring self efficacy in teaching. Within the school, teachers need to discuss ways of improving the mathematics curriculum. Learning from each other is vital such as meeting together to discuss results from standardized tests. Feedback should aid in improving learner achievement.
- improvement in parent/teacher conferences assists in securing input on ways of helping learner mathematical performance. Quality standards must be used in these conferences in truly obtaining information from parents in cooperatively guiding pupil achievement. Good human relations needs to be in the offing whereby

parents feel welcome and engaged during the conference. A portfolio of the pupil's actual work products may provide an excellent basis for a conference whereby the parent may see actual work completed by the learner in mathematics.

- problem solving emphasizes cooperative endeavors among teachers in stressing the following to optimize pupil mathematics progress:
  (1) working together to attain objectives of the curriculum
  (2) emphasizing good human relations in order to develop positive attitudes
  (3) eliminate rude remarks; these hinder achievement and progress
  (4) encourage all to participate, no one dominate
  (5) stay on the topic being pursued.
- advocate the community school concept whereby all in a given region are involved in improving the school curriculum. This aids in developing the academic discipline of mathematics as well as the other areas of the curriculum. Getting communities to accept and promote the community school concept takes time and incremental increases will come about as the school years progress. Each teacher, school administrator, as well as support faculty member, must be actively involved in being a promotor of public school education.

REFERENCES

Ediger, Marlow (2008), "Modern School Mathematics", *College Student Journal*, 42 (4), 986-989.

Ediger, Marlow, and D. Bhaskara Rao (2011), *Essays in Teaching Mathematics*. New Delhi, India: Discovery Publishing House Ltd.

Vygotsky, Len (1978), *Mind in Society, The Development of Higher Mental Processes*. Cambridge, Massachusetts; Harvard University Press.

Collaboration in Improving the Mathematics Curriculum

By working together mathematics teachers and supervisors can do much to improve teaching and learning in mathematics. Collaboration is important to develop high quality objectives, learning opportunities and appraisal procedures in teaching pupils. Each participant needs to be well informed of recommended procedures, research and technology in instructional settings.

A special section in the school library needs to house instructional materials for mathematics teachers. Thus, university level teaching of mathematics textbooks, professional mathematics teaching journals, different series of math textbooks K-12, video tapes on mathematics instruction, among other references sources need to be available for teacher referral and use.

Curriculum Improvement in Mathematics

With the team approach, participants may share ideas and engage in higher levels of cognition to solve problems in teaching mathematics. There are a plethora of points of intervention. First, the objectives of instruction need scrutiny in terms of raising the following questions:

- Are the objectives relevant for learners in school and in society, as well as for those going into the professions?
- Do they stress a balance between subject matter knowledge and skills in mathematics?

- Are they arranged sequentially in moving from what is taught and understood to those which are gradually more complex?
- Is meaning making and deriving sense in ensuing mathematical lessons being emphasized?
- Are attitudinal objectives being stressed adequately?

Collaboration in studying and evaluating objectives in mathematics is time well spent. The objectives need to possess clarity and stated in measurable terms so that it may be ascertained if, after instruction, they have been attained by pupils. Periodical review of what is taught leads to a better understanding of what pupils are experiencing and which innovations need to be advocated. With collaboration, mathematics teachers might well try out revised objectives in their classrooms and report back to the group how well teaching and learning transpired. Problems identified here need study and recommendations made to further improve the mathematics curriculum.

Learning opportunities for pupils to achieve the objectives also need indepth study by participants in collaborative endeavors. Learning opportunities must be varied to provide for each pupil so that he/she may attain as optimally as possible. Different kinds of learning opportunities need to be discussed to determine what works and what changes/ modifications need to be made. Active participation in collaborative endeavors may be fostered by paying attention to *relevant,* not trivial, items in teaching and learning situations. Video tapes of classroom teaching might well provide a basis for analyzing teacher and pupil behaviors in mathematical units of study. The following identified problem areas need consideration:

- What should be the role of the latest in technology in the math curriculum?
- Must inservice education be emphasized to assist mathematics teachers to fully utilize technology to assist pupils in meaningful leanings?

- Which additional kinds of technology, than those possessed, are necessary to aid in the instructional arena?
- Would an increased use of technology stimulate pupil interest in ongoing experiences in the classroom?
- What is the role of more traditional procedures in teaching such as carefully chosen textbooks, workbooks, and work sheets?

The mathematics teacher models quality attitudes toward content, skills and an appreciation for efforts made by mathematicians in developing knowledge and skills in the mathematical arena. It is vital for teachers to keep up with the latest developments in the teaching of mathematics. Technology continues to come out at a rapid rate and teachers must be aware of what will assist pupils to do well in math achievement. Learning by discovery, problem solving, as well as creative and critical thinking need to permeate the math curriculum.

Collaboration by teachers in assessing pupil achievement is vital. Certainly, a quality assessment program is necessary. With standardized testing, math teachers need to attach meaning to the following concepts pertaining to assessment:

- validity of the test and how its is determined
- reliability and its role in the development of tests
- the definition of standardized tests
- formative and summative evaluation as well as measuring benchmarks of pupil progress
- accompanying Manual and its uses.

Teacher written tests are salient to use at selected intervals to measure achievement. Multiple choice test items should possess the following standards:

- each test item should generally have four distractors.
- the distractors should be of simulator length so that clues are minimized/eliminated as to the correct response.
- the stem and each of the four distractors should make for a grammatically correct sentence.

- no pattern should exist in terms of which is the correct response.

Face validity may be used when writing teacher written tests. Thus, after a concept or generalization has been taught, the mathematics teacher may then apply the same content in writing a test item. Clarity and meaning must be inherent in each test item written. Few teachers use test/retest approaches to check reliability. *Reliability* emphasizes that a test measure consistently. Test/retest reliability means giving the same test two times within a few days apart to notice if learners, basically, received the same/similar percentile or number of correct test responses. If the scores differ much from one testing to the next for the same pupil, the chances are the test times are vague or do not measure what was taught, among other factors. *Alternative forms reliability* emphasizes the mathematics teacher write two separate tests covering objectives in the lesson or unit of study taught. Teachers generally do not have the needed time to do this. However, split half reliability requires administering the teacher written test once, and then comparing the even numbered with the odd numbered responses for all pupils in a class. Does the test measure consistently in that generally Pupil A is highest in both the odd/even comparison; pupil B is second high whereas pupil C is third high, and so on.

Teacher written *essay* test items may do a good job of assessing mathematics achievement if selected criteria are met such as the following:

- the items are written on the understanding level of pupils. If reading is a problem, the teacher may read the test items aloud. The writer when teaching in a two teacher rural school had two seventh graders in one grade level only. It did not take long to notice that reading caused difficulties in solving word problems; these were then read aloud to the two pupils who then did fairly well on the arithmetic facet.
- essay test items need to be delimited, but not to the point of requiring factual answers. Thus, a problem

solving approach is recommenced whereby pupils need to deliberate and think to ascertain answers. Problems in mathematics need to involve indepth thought in which critical and creative thinking are involved.

- the test length should measure objectives stressed in class, but not to the length whereby learner fatigue sets in when responding. The purpose is to measure mathematical problem solving skills and not endurance.
- pupils may show procedures used in problem solving. Mathematics teachers might then view how pupils responded as well as the answer obtained. This provides feedback to the teacher as to what needs reteaching and emphasis necessary to optimize pupil achievement.

There are additional avenues of collaborative thinking in improving teacher evaluation in the mathematics curriculum. These include teacher observation of learner performance. Collaboration here must stress how observation of pupils in ongoing math lessons and units of study can be made more effective. The following should be considered carefully:

- examples of knowledge to be used in highly specific procedures to solve mathematical problems. Indepth math knowledge needs to be used here. Too frequently, this may be lacking when arriving at a solution.
- ways of assisting pupils to learn inductively.
- emphasizing mathematical reasoning in observations made.
- recording dated observations and summarizing results.
- filing observational data for each pupil to be used in making subsequent comparisons.

There are a plethora of means to use collaborative thinking in the mathematics curriculum. Working together harmoniously, mathematics teachers may collaboratively solve problems pertaining to objectives, learning opportunities and appraisal procedures.

Chapter 27 Improving the Mathematics Curriculum

Instruction in the teaching of mathematics will require the best curriculum possible for pupils in the school setting. The common core standards emphasize college/career readiness, starting with the primary grade levels. Each level of achievement will build upon what pupils have acquired previously in going from the known to the unknown in a sequential manner. Upgrading the mathematics curriculum to a more challenging level is desirable when motivating learners to make optimal progress.

Motivating Pupil Achievement

Beginning with the kindergarten level, the mathematics teacher needs to emphasize background learnings which will provide a sturdy foundation in whole numbers, the four basic operations, fractions and decimals. This will provide subject matter, necessary to understand increasingly more complex facts, concepts, and generalizations. Teachers need to be certain that each pupil attaches meaning in each sequential step of learning. It is vital that learners understand and can demonstrate that objectives have been attained. If rote learning occurs only, then pupils are not ready for the ensuing activity in mathematics. With careful observation of achievement, the teacher might well ascertain if an objective has been attained by each pupil. This will assist learners to achieve more optimally in the common core standards. Pupil interest needs to be developed/maintained throughout each lesson so that active engagement in learning in evidence. No pupil should fall through the cracks, but rather assisted where difficulties and problems are faced.

Perseverance is a salient trait for pupils to attain. Too frequently, a pupil may desire to give up when a difficulty is faced in an ongoing lesson. Wise encouragement must be meted out by the teacher for pupils to achieve success. Here, the concept of scaffolding becomes significant. The mathematics teacher then helps a pupil to build on what is known and then assists in realizing an objective which seemingly is too complex at the present time. This is done with questions raised by the teacher and brief explanations provided to guide the learner in achieving the more complex objective. Pupils like to realize they can "stretch their minds" with more challenging learnings in mathematics. Well prepared math teachers possess diverse strategies and content in guiding sequential learner achievement when scaffolding is utilized in teaching and learning situations. Scaffolding aids pupils to persevere and progress in attaining common core learnings.

Readiness for attaining ensuing objectives needs careful consideration. Having high quality experiences in mathematics is needed for pupils to achieve well in concepts stressing algebra, geometry, probability, as well as statistics. Mathematics teachers must pay careful attention to the order of learnings presented so that a seamless curriculum comes about. If this is lacking, diagnosis and remediation might be necessary since pupils will experience more difficulties at specific points in a lesson presentation. Teachers should provide ample opportunities for pupils to meet in small groups to discuss problems faced in mathematics. This provides facets of inservice education for teachers. Additional procedures of inservice mathematical education include workshops, departmental meetings, attending state and national conventions, doing an independent study, taking college/ university courses and participating in seminars. A competent teacher can do much to assist pupils in attaining, growing, and achieving. Readiness for learning indicates a pupil might well benefit much from new learnings presented and challenging mathematical subject matter in the common core might well be acquired through scaffolding.

When subject matter is too complicated, pupils might become frustrated and put forth little effort. Thus, a knowledgeable teacher will observe pupils carefully to notice negative effaces of selected endeavors. Good and positive attitudes toward mathematics are salient. Quality attitudes aids in achieving relevant common core objectives. There is an attitudinal dimension which must be fostered and this is resilience. When supervising university student teachers in the public schools, the writer observed pupils who give up readily, particularly in problem solving experiences. By giving sequential assistance and encouragement, pupils are assisted in bouncing back (resilience) to complete each problem. The assistance may remediate a lack of meaning attached to the problem when it just does not make sense. It is good if the math teacher takes time to guide learners in perceiving relevance in the problem and how these are useful learnings in society. Life consists of difficulties faced and these need to be solved as problems not as situations involving abandoning a task. Math teachers and pupils must look at these situations as room for growth, rather than despair; learnings accrue from problematic occurrences. Thus, pupils need to develop feelings of resilience instead of hopelessness. Common core objectives, then, have a better chance of their achievement.

Interest in learning is paramount and makes for wholehearted engagement in mathematical tasks. Learning experiences involving thinking makes for interest in achievement. Thus, for example, a collaborative endeavor in which a small group of pupils engage in solving a problem in mathematics might well reveal the following kinds of thinking:

- logical thought which is a major category in math.
- critical thinking-separating facts from opinions, important from unimportant ideas, as well as relevant from irrelevant content.

- creative thinking in coming up with unique, new ideas, for example, in determining a more suitable algorithm.
- structural subject matter as in the commutative, associative and distributive properties.
- perceiving patterns as in the set of counting numbers.
- inferential thinking as in generalizing for a given set of data.
- formative evaluation should be utilized to ascertain what pupils have left to learn within daily lessons or units of study. It provides feedback in providing quality sequence in achievement. Summative evaluate is end of unit appraisal to notice how well pupils have done when culmination occurs. Plans then need to be made to make modifications and necessary changes in the math curriculum within the completed unit of study.

In Conclusion

There are a plethora of facts, concepts and generalizations which might well be inherent in a quality mathematics curriculum. Accurate subject matter knowledge is a necessity for teachers. Inservice education is needed to keep abreast with the latest content. Appropriate methodology must be utilized to assist pupils to attain more optimally; each pupil needs to achieve well and not fall through the cracks. Salient technology must be available and used appropriately in teaching and learning situations. Technology should be useful to guide/propel progression and not utilized for its own sake. Technology needs to be embedded in the math curriculum which fosters specific and generalized learning. A variety of learning opportunities assists in providing for individual differences among learners. Optimizing success for each pupil ensures more adequate motivation, as well as provision made for diverse styles of learning. The common core standards must guide pupils to do well in mathematics.

Poetry in the Mathematics Curriculum

Mathematics teachers are always on the lookout for creative endeavours which will also reinforce pupil subject matter and skills acquired. Novelty, too, is then introduced into the curriculum which provides for variation in teaching and learning situations. A variety of purposeful experiences tends to minimize boredom in ongoing activities. The writer when supervising university student teachers in the public schools observed on different occasions whereby the student teacher and the cooperating teacher as a team taught mathematical poetry to pupils in ongoing units of study. There was seemingly considerable excitement in pupil engagement.

Poetry and Mathematics

Diverse kinds of poetry may be written. Working as a team, the cooperating and student teacher, taught pupils rhyme in verse. Thus, for example, a couplet has two lines with ending words rhyming. Pupils experiment with words in creating rhyme. Clues may be provided by the teacher if learners are stymied which happens rarely in developing a couplet. If pupils are too young to do their very own writing, the teacher may copy what has been dictated by pupils. For the class as a whole to do the composing, the teacher may write what pupils have said orally. Within a small collaborative group, one pupil might be designated to do the writing, or pupils may write their very own poem. Additional verse containing rhyme include the following:

- A triplet has three lines with ending words rhyming and may be written by young children and older, when readiness is in evidence.
- A quatrain has four lines with all ending words rhyming or lines one and two rhyme with lines three and four also containing rhyme.
- A limerick has five lines with lines one, two and five rhyming as well as lines three and four containing rhyme. Limericks generally begin with the words, "There once was..." However, each described poem above may be modified in developing novelty in thinking.

Many pupils enjoy rhyme in poetry and models may be provided by the teacher reading rhymed verse to learners and/or pupils reading rhyme in poetry. In mathematics, the goals is for learners to inject mathematical subject matter into the kinds of poetry written. The emphasis is upon pupils utilizing subject matter acquired (Ediger and Rao, 2011). Poetry without rhyme comes in a variety of forms and most are written as non-rhyming. Motivation is high and interest intense when pupils write poems without rhyme in mathematics. The following free verse was written with collaboration by a small group of sixth graders in an ongoing mathematical unit of study:

Arithmetic involves
 Addition, subtraction, multiplication and division
 Carrying, regrouping, and renaming
 Thinking, problem solving, logic and concentration
 Reading, writing, speaking and listening.

The above listed free verse may be extended. Pupils do reveal their understanding of arithmetic in poetry writing. The ingredients which go into a poem requires brain storming and continuous evaluation.

Writing acrostic verse might well fascinate selected learners.

This, too, may emphasize small group, the class as a whole, or individual endeavors. An single word may be taken from a mathematics unit of study and each letter of that word written horizontally. For each letter, The following was written by a pupil individually with the concept geometry being utilized:

G. . . . geometry in motion

e. . . . eager to learn

o. . . . on task

m. . . . measurement

e. . . . equations

t. . . . triangle

r. . . . right angle

y. . . . yearning to succeed.

Here, learners need to focus upon the title and bring to bear words which are relevant and indicative of geometry. Brain storming and higher levels of cognition are involved when learners come up with creative responses in developing the poem. Creativity is present when pupils pursue the novel, the unique, and that which is original. All attempts made by pupils must be respected so that creative thinking is not stymied. Once ridicule and rudeness set in, selected pupils cease to contribute. If a pupil attempts to be "silly" in giving responses, the teacher may ask, among other approaches, "if this really fits in with the title of geometry? Reading and writing poetry should be enjoyable as well as motivating.

A rather complex type of poem to compose is the diamante. Diamantes are diamond shaped and may be quite meaningful to learners. All poems should have a title and in the case of the diamante is an noun or object. If students are studying a statistic unit of study, the title might well be Statistics. Line two needs to have two words (adjectives) which describe the object or noun—significant level; line three has three "ing" ending words (participles) which describe the title of the diamante—working, writing, succeeding. Line four has four nouns directly related to the title—mean, mode, median, delimitation. Line four emphasizes the wide part or width of the diamond shaped diamante. Line five emphasizes three "ing" ending words (participles) which modify line four of the diamante. These might be the following: averaging, graphing, counting. This is followed by two adjectives describing the title (subject) of the diamante: skewness, curve. The last line has one word which forms the base of the diamante and tells about the title (subject) – data.

The entire diamond appears as in the following figure:

Statistics
significant level
working, writing, succeeding
mean, mode, median, delimitation
averaging, graphing, counting
skewness, curve
data

The above named diamante assists learners to concentrate on relevant concepts in an ongoing high school unit of study involving statistics. Much information is presented in statistical form in the printed news media. Readers of statistical information must be informed in how to read and interpret the data. Creativity occurs in all academic areas (Ranganath, 2012).

REFERENCES

Ediger, Marlow and D. Bhaskara Rao (2011), *Essays in Teaching Mathematics*. New Delhi, India: Discovery Publishing House Ltd.

Ranganath, A. (2012), "A Study of Creativity, Scientific Attitude and Attitudes Towards the Science of Perspective Science Teachers of Andhra Pradesh". Ph.D. thesis evaluated by Marlow Ediger for Acharya Nagarjuna University, India, Ranganath has completed his docteral thesis in Education under the guidance of Digumarti Bhaskara Rao.

Reading in the Mathematics Curriculum

There are selected procedures which may be used to assist students having difficulties in reading mathematics problems. Difficulties in reading should not hold students back from achieving more optimally in mathematics. Methods of helping students with reading problems and comprehension in mathematics will be discussed in this manuscript.

Analyzing Mathematical Reading Problems

Several procedures will be discussed. The teacher may immediately pronounce words to a student who fail in the identification process. This procedure has as its advantage in that students will not lose out on ideas read due to the almost immediate pronunciation of unknown words in context. However, the student may not retain these as sight words if no specific approach is learned in word recognition (Ediger, 2007).

Phonics might well assist students in reading an unknown word. The word "sum" is very consistent in spelling between symbol and sound. Phonics works very well in word identification when words reveal this consistency. With other words in mathematics, there is less consistency such as in the following: "greater" than, "inverse" operation, "regroup," "subtraction," among others. Even in these words there is some consistency as in "gr," (group), inverse without its "in" prefix, "regroup," with "re" prefix consistency between symbol and sound, as well as "subtraction" with "sub" letters, each making its very own consistent sound.

Irregularly spelled words may be recognized as following a pattern such as "tion" in the words subtraction, addition, and multiplication, making the ending sound of "shun." If phonics does not work in word recognition, then context clues might well assist. Thus, words must fit in meaningfully with the balance of the words in the sentence or paragraph. Sometimes, students fill in words which just do not make sense. The word must make for meaningful learning (Ediger, 1989).

Recognizing known syllables has many advantages in unlocking unknown words. If a student does not recognize a word, he/she may divide it into syllables for identification purposes, making the word(s) recognizable. The prefix "un" is used frequently as is the suffix "er." By removing a syllable, then, a pupil may identify a word correctly.

As a junior high school teacher, the writer in the latter fifties read aloud several word problems while struggling readers in *a* small group would follow along in their mathematics textbooks. This was done in an atmosphere of respect for all in the classroom. Struggling readers, generally could then proceed sequentially with the usual amount of supervision.

Reading Mathematics Problems Aloud

As a method of tackling problems in word recognition then, the writer read aloud selected story problems as the struggling readers followed along in their textbooks. In this way, learners were able to do the needed work in mathematics. Also, an opaque projector may be used to enlarge the print from the basal textbook so all can see clearly from their seats in a small group. The teacher may then read the words aloud as students follow along from the screen. Next, students may read aloud together with the teacher until the read aloud is successful and students understand what to do in mathematics. This approach does not embarrass any slow reader. Problems In reading should not interfere with achievement in mathematics. How did this assist learners?

- pupils developed a basic mathematics sight vocabulary from repeated reading.
- pupils decide which words should then appear on a word wall, for review purposes.
- pupils should comprehend the ideas well from the read aloud.
- pupils develop a better self-concept by not stumbling on word recognition problems (See National Council Teachers of Mathematics, 1989).

Peer reading of word problems my also be emphasized. Thus, a proficient reader may read aloud to others who have difficulties in word recognition. In an atmosphere of respect, he/she needs to read aloud so that word identification does not hinder achievement in mathematics. The writer has noticed in classrooms whereby lay volunteers do a good job of helping students to decode and understand word problems. A conscientious Future Teachers of America high school club member has been observed to do a very good job of assisting struggling readers to identify unknown words (Ediger, 2007).

A variety of interesting procedures need to be used to assist struggling readers to identify unknown words. Methods of word recognition must be quickly implemented so that students secure the needed mathematical information sequentially to solve word problems. Being stuck on unknown words makes for feelings of failure. Sequence of ideas in reading then comes to a halt with frustration involved. Rather, assistance needs to be given quickly in word identification so that the learner may attend to solving mathematical problems, rather than struggling over unknown words.

There are salient principles of psychology which the mathematics teacher should use when assisting students in word recognition. These include the following:

- engaging students in learning rather than have passive recipients of knowledge.
- providing adequate background information to students, prior to proceeding with the unknown.

- emphasize meaning and understanding in teaching and learning situations.
- stress interest factors in learning; avoid student boredom in achieving.
- assist students to perceive purpose in identifying unknown words (See Roy, 2009).

Providing for Individual Needs

Mathematics teachers need to provide for individual differences among students. Thus, needs vary from student to student. With diagnosis and remediation data, the teacher may assist each to achieve more optimally in mathematics. Mathematics must be taught from a developmental point of view, but this is not always possible. Thus, the teacher needs to analyze what pupils need and then strengthen these areas of concern.

Mathematics teachers need to ascertain where a pupil is achieving presently and then provide quality experiences which make for subsequent feelings of accomplishment. The materials of instruction used might well provide for individual styles of learning also, such as the utilization of:

- concrete objects and items to teach addition, subtraction, multiplication, and division, *i.e.* checkers used to show a set of five and set of three, joining the two sets to make a set of eight. The abstract numerals "5+3=8" should accompany the concrete markers. Structural ideas including the commutative property of addition and multiplication, the associative property of addition and multiplication. The inverse operation of subtraction and division may also be shown with concrete markers and the accompanying abstract numerals.
- semi-concrete materials to convey mathematical including pictures, illustrations, audio-visual aids, power point slides, teacher made felt cut outs and the flannel board, diagrams and drawings, and video tapes explaining salient mathematics procedures and processes.

- abstract materials of instruction including the mathematics basal textbook, the number line, related worksheets and the accompanying workbook, computer use, as well as teacher developed materials (See Kennedy and Tipps, 1991).

Each of the above must be adapted to individual pupil needs such as pupils reading content from pictures and illustrations in assisting pupils in learning to count drawings therein. Or, accompanying work book subject matter used to determine the area of a parallelogram.

Methods of teaching must match the learning styles of pupils, in general and these include the following:

- inductive learning or learning by discovery in mathematics.
- deductive learning through clearly provided explanations.
- project methods as in developing a *product* such as a triangle, square, trapezoid and rectangle from construction paper.
- problem solving in which a small group or committee of pupils seek to find solutions to a lifelike mathematical problem whereby higher cognitive levels of thought are used in the process.

Conclusion

There are a variety of purposes involved in reading mathematical content. Word recognition and comprehension are two vital factors in reading mathematical subject matter. Pupils must attach meaning to what is being read so that they may work on the mathematical facets of computing, reasoning, and understanding.

REFERENCES

Ediger, Marlow (1989), "Psychology of Teaching Mathematics," *Delta K*, 27 (4), 20-23.

Ediger, Marlow (2007), "Meaning in Reading Instruction," *Reading Improvement*, 44(4), 217-220.

Ediger, Marlow (2007), "Readiness for Mathematics Learning and the Student," *Experiments in Education*, 35 (8), 1-5.

National Council Teachers of Mathematics (1989), *Curriculum and Evaluation Standards for School Mathematics.* Reston, Virginia: NCTM.

Roy, Ruma (2009), "New Challenges in Teacher Education", *Edutracks*, 8 (6), 19-20.

Kennedy, Leonard M., Tipps, Steve (1991), *Guiding Children's Learning of Mathematics*. Belmont, California: Wadsworth Publishing Company.

Pointers in Teaching Mathematics

There are selected criteria for mathematics teachers to follow which assist pupils to achieve more optimally. These criteria follow recommended principles of psychology in teaching and learning. They become salient pointers in teaching mathematics.

First, teachers must help pupils to become actively engaged in ongoing lessons and units of study. If pupils fail to be involved, they are not focusing on key or subordinate ideas in mathematics. Lessons tend to build on each other in facts, concepts and generalizations, and if pupils do not attend carefully, quality logical sequence will be lacking.

Second, pupils possess their individual styles of learning. As much as possible, these must enter into the equation for planning of effective instruction. The following considerations then are salient:

- individual activities as compared to committee endeavors, each to be considered important in providing for individual differences.
- materials of teaching differentiated such as the concrete, consisting of diverse objects and items; the semi-concrete such as power point, computerized items; illustrations and the pictorial, as well as the abstract (materials in print form). These need variation in providing for different levels of instruction among learners.

- methods of grouping for teaching and learning (large group or small group, homogeneously or heterogeneously grouped) Through teacher observation, pupils may be observed carefully in order to provide immediate attention to errors made and then followed by remediation. Teacher written tests and standardized tests need to possess high validity and reliability in providing for quality results in evaluation which provide feedback for instruction.

Pupils need to experience meaningful learnings. Thus, learners must make sense of what is taught and presented in mathematics. If content is meaningless, pupils will not be able to perform proficiently on the ensuing subject matter. New facts, concepts and generalizations are related to previously learned subject matter. Critical and creative thinking as well as problem solving aid in understanding mathematical content. Above all else, the mathematics teacher must be well prepared for each lesson presented. Inservice educa-tion is continually necessary to remain current in teaching and learning situations. Thus, securing a graduate degree, attending state and national conventions dealing with mathematics instruction, as well as reading and thinking about content read in the teaching of mathematics from leading journals and teacher education textbooks, help to make for self efficacy and professionalism in mathematics instruction (Ediger and Rao, 2011).

REFERENCE

Ediger, Marlow and D. Bhaskara Rao (2011), Essays in Teaching Mathematics. New Delhi, India: Discovery Publishing House Ltd.

The Psychology of Learning in Teaching Mathematics

The mathematics teacher has a plethora of ingredients to emphasize in teaching and learning situations. First of all, having breadth and depth of knowledge to use in the instructional arena is salient. Bringing in available technology to improve pupil learning is a must in ongoing experiences. These need blending with the psychology of learning in assisting pupils to attain as optimally as possible. It is vital then to secure the interests of learners in ongoing experiences. Without the interest factor, pupil involvement will be more minimal. Learning activities to achieve objectives need to be varied, challenging, and on the ability levels of learners. It behooves the teacher to choose and select those experiences which develop and maintain interest factors. Additional criteria for teaching mathematics also need attention (See National Council Teachers of Mathematics, 1989).

Quality in Teaching Mathematics

Motivation of pupils in attaining mathematics objectives means that the energy level increases for achievement. Motivated pupils are attentive and eager to participate actively in the curriculum. On task behavior is there with the attention span increased and not spent on day dreaming, or what will be done during the week end. The mathematics teacher needs to observe pupils to notice achievement as well as where diagnosis and remediation are necessary. Meticulous observation of learners in the classroom setting provides feedback for teaching as well as opportunities for teachers to get to know pupil behavior better in seeking new, innovative ways to motivate. Creative approaches must be found to increase pupil motivation in the mathematics curriculum (Ediger and Rao, 2011).

Second, meaning in each learning in mathematics must be emphasized. Those facts, concepts and generalizations acquired provide building blocks for ensuing lessons. If there are hazy learnings, the chances are pupils will experience difficulties with new objectives to be secured. A professional teacher possesses a reservoir of mathematical knowledge and skills in guiding pupils to overcome problem areas. Content acquired must make sense and be understood clearly. The teacher needs to pace subject matter in a manner which facilitates achievement of objectives. The goal here is for pupils to master vital subject matter and abilities (critical and creative thinking, reasoning skills, as well as problem solving, among others) to perform satisfactorily.

Third, purpose needs to be stressed and accepted by pupils in ongoing lessons. Thus, pupils acquire reasons for participating actively. With purpose learners perceive a need for utilizing subject matter in school and in society. Mathematics is functional, precise and contains patterns for mastery. Too frequently, pupils see mathematics as another day of drill and rote learning. Rather, it must be perceived as being exciting in making discoveries and be challenging. When observing pupils in the classroom, too often, learners are perceives as lethargic and disinterested. It should be just the opposite, with active participation and use of manipulative materials, among others, which harmonize with the developmental level of those in the classroom. Methods of teaching utilized make it possible to adjust the curriculum to where pupils are presently and then sequence leanings to make for continuous progress (See Wiske, 2004).

Fourth, resilience must be integrated into the mathematics curricula. With resilience, pupils "bounce back" when experiencing difficulties and failures. A major problem in teaching is that learners give up too quickly in problem solving activities as well as when a new process is being emphasized. Securing pupil attention is salient and careful order of steps in teaching new learnings is necessary so that individuals might well be successful in achievement. However, in school and in society, frustrating situations do occur. Pupils need assistance in dealing with these difficulties in a manner which stresses resilience. One procedure is for the teacher to scaffold subject matter content and skills. A competent math teacher then might well raise sequential questions of the learner whereby he/ she discovers the answer or knowledge to realize an increased difficult objective. Instead of an inductive approach, the teacher, deductively, might sequence from where the child is having difficulty to the desired level of accomplishment. This, too, can make for feelings of accomplishment as well as minimize frustration, with chances of success in future endeavors.

Fifth, the teacher must be accountable for behaviors exhibited. Off the cuff statements in a moment of weakness may be costly in terms of receiving a recommend, or even being dismissed. Calling students negative names or losing one's temper might be extremely regrettable. Harassment and rudeness must be eliminated from the school setting. The consequences of doing things in a negative way be high indeed. It behooves the teacher to be in complete control of his/her actions. Emotional intelligence is needed by teachers to control one's behavior and actions. Probably, all have been in classes along the way from elementary school through the college years whereby an instructor lost his/her temper for one reason or another. Teaching can be very stressful and the teacher mast be aware of being accountable in exhibiting positive behavior, such as in the following situations:

- selected pupils disrupting teaching in ongoing lessons.
- learners failing to get it in specific mathematical processes being explained.
- pupil behavior *not* being focused on subject matter/ skills presented.

- the classroom atmosphere lacking in attempting to promote learning.

It is not easy to deal with one's emotions in difficult stations, but it is imperative that the responsibility rests with the teacher in achieving a positive learning environment. Otherwise, learner achievement in mathematics will tend to go downhill. Teachers must learn about the customs, mores, and folkways of a given community in order to understand beliefs, and motivational patterns of pupils. The total child is involved in learning, not the academic and cognitive facets alone or largely. Each has diverse needs which must be fulfilled. Some of these, the school can fulfill such as providing breakfasts, lunches, as well as take home food for the weekend. There are still hunger needs to be met with dinner; a few schools have remedied this situation by serving dinner after selected play activities have been completed at the end of a school day. All teachers must attempt to involve learners in meeting belonging needs. Collaborative and committee endeavours in which learners work harmoniously together is a starting point here. Being an isolate greatly hinders pupil progress in mathematics as well as in other curriculum areas.

In Conclusion

Mathematics teachers need to possess self-efficacy in knowledge to impart to pupils. Knowledge here consists of relevant facts, concepts and generalizations, necessary for high quality instruction. These are needed for a developmental approach in sequencing learnings for pupils. Subject matter knowledge, alone, is not adequate. The mathematics teacher must also be able to utilize the best of methodology possible to reach children's abilities in teaching and learning situations. High expectations, but achievable objectives should be in the offing. Scaffolding needs to be used when assisting learners to realize optimal achievement. Appraisal of learner progress must be continuous with the use of feedback to improve the curriculum. Inservice education is necessary to stay abreast of current developments in instruction, such as the ensuing common core objectives.

REFERENCES

Ediger, Marlow and D. Bhaskara Rao (2011), *Essays in Teaching Mathematics*, New Delhi, India; Discovery Publishing House.

National Council Teachers of Mathematics (1989), *Curriculum and Evaluation Standards for School Mathematics.* Reston, Virginia; NCTM.

Wiske, S. (2004), "Technology to dig for Meaning," *Educational Leadership*, 62(1), 478.

Relevancy in Mathematics

Teachers needs to stress what is relevant and vital in mathematics. Too frequently, the unimportant and what can be memorized quickly for testing purposes is emphasized. Mathematics teachers need to meet together and collaboratively weed out what is not salient and pinpoint important concepts and generalizations for teaching in ongoing units of study. Thus, the Common Core State Standards (CESS) might well provide guidance and direction.

Important Learnings in Mathematics

For important objectives to emphasize, lifelong learning in mathematics should become a central objective for all to attain. This will come in degrees in continuous growth and development throughout one's life time, not in a single endeavour. Interest then becomes a key factor. Thus in the classroom, the mathematics teacher must plan activities to capture learner interest in sequential ongoing units of study. Wholehearted involvement by all pupils means that the teacher must teach what is relevant and salient as well as secure the attention of each pupil in teaching and learning situations. Within this framework, mathematics teachers may devise new lessons and units of study which are based upon that which learners have acquired previously. Jumping to far ahead of pupils in presenting subject matter content might well be frustrating to pupils whereas content which is too easy and has already been mastered might well be boring to most in the classroom setting. It behooves the teacher then to develop as seamlessly as possible within the pupil, the new subject matter with previously acquired concepts and generalizations. Pupils success in achieving optimally is of utmost importance (Ediger and Rao, 2011)!

Pupils, too, must perceive *purpose* in participating in a given mathematical process involving subject matter and skills. Thus, the teacher inductively/deductively needs to assist learners to realize the saliency of pursuing a new objective or the necessity of reviewing previous learnings. Then, too, there is a need to ascertain "why" a problem was solved incorrectly or basic numerical facts were not computed correctly. Thus, it is highly important for pupils to understand purpose in an ongoing lesson. Generally, as adults, something is done in society due to the purpose involved, not for the sake of doing so.

Different Levels of Thinking

Pupils need to engage in diverse levels of thought in performing different operations on number. Memorizing the answers to basic number pairs is the lowest level of cognition. It is important for pupils to understand the answers to basic number pairs in addition, subtraction, multiplication, and division, but it must move upward to understanding what each equals to and this includes comprehension. Meaning in acquisition of mathematical learnings is significant. Mathematics has its own unique vocabulary and each term must be meaningful. Concrete, semi-concrete and abstract learnings are important here. Comprehension of vocabulary terms is salient in working with and the utilization of these in functional settings. Life in society demands that this be done in daily transactions performed.

Critical thinking is then involved when pupils are guided to separate facts from opinions. Mathematics is precise and lends itself to objectivity in thought. Answers to lifelike problems can be verified. The writer was always amused when selected students in his graduate classes came up with an incorrect answer to $3 + 4 \times 5 + 2$. The "x" means times and this operation is performed prior to any addition and subtraction operations 3 + (4 × 5) + 2 when responding to its value. Rules must be followed here pertaining to multiplication and addition in this problem and learners can be shown why these rules are important; when going strictly from left to right, the answer is different as compared to following the rule of multiplication coming before addition in the above example of 3 + 4 × 5 + 2. Critical thinking is involved in solving word problems in that that what is needed is separated from that which does not aid in solving the problem. Then too, the order of operations must be determined, especially in solving multi-step problems. Thus in critical thinking, for example, the important must be separated from the unimportant, as well as what is vital must be ascertained. Too frequently, pupils may not attach meaning to the word problem and approach solutions haphazardly by adding, subtracting, multiplying, and dividing numerals given, in the word problem, in any random order.

Creative thought is also salient in that novel, unique approaches need to be found which aid the learner in becoming increasingly proficient in mathematics. For instance, the learner may discover a new algorithm for himself/herself, in problem solving which is beneficial. In geometry, as an additional example in creativity, pupils individually or collectively, might well develop original designs, among others, with the use of a compass and protractor in an ongoing unit of study.

Developing appropriate reading skills in mathematics is highly important as well as relevant. In using context clues to identify unknown words plus significant leanings in phonics, the pupil may become quite independent in word recognition skills. The teacher or a skilled reader might well assist additionally, the point being that the learner should understand abstract words read as well as mathematical symbols. Meaning helps to make subject matter relevant and useful.

REFERENCE

Ediger, Marlow and D. Bhaskara Rao (2011), *Essays In Teaching Mathematics*. New Delhi, India: Discovery Publishing House Ltd.

Data Driven Decision-making in Mathematics

Of all academic areas in the curriculum, data driven decision-making works best in mathematics due to its preciseness and patterns possessed. In data driven instruction, the mathematics teacher needs to develop specific objectives which leaves little/no leeway for interpretation. The teacher teaches so that pupils attain these objectives with learning activities which possess:

- purpose or logical reasons for their use.
- interest which propels learners to achieve goals.
- meaning so that pupils understand indepth what is taught (Ediger, 1989).

After instruction, the math teacher may measure if pupils have achieved these objectives. Those not achieved by learners provide ensuing objectives and learning opportunities for goal attainment. There are diverse mathematics tests which may be used to document pupil progress.

Testing to Notice Achievement

Mandated mathematics tests have become exceedingly important in society. These may be state or district wide tests. Statewide tests tend to be standardized in that a commercial company developed the items for testing purposes, generally multiple choice in nature. The tests are standardized in that they contain the same content, the same directions for test taking and the same time limits for that age level of pupils talking the test. To standardize the mathematics test, pilot studies were run to a random sample of pupils. The results were then categorized into norms for the standardized test. A pupil's results from presently taking the test are then compared to the norm group in order to secure percentile, and/or grade and age level equivalent information (See Newton, 2007).

The Manual of the standardized test indicates how the test items were validated. Any standardized test must be valid. Thus if the involved math teacher wishes to measure pupil achievement in the basic four operations on number of addition, subtraction, multiplication, and division, then the standardized test must measure pupils achievement in these four operations to be valid. They will be written for a specific age or grade level. Reliability, also, is salient in that a standardized test must measure consistently. Thus if a fourth grader receives a test result of being on the fortieth percentile, he/she should receive approximately the fortieth percentile on the second time the test is taken. This is test/retest reliability. If pupils are tested once, the odd numbered versus the even numbered test items should produce similar results for many pupils, in order for the test to be reliable. This method can be used with teacher written classroom tests since one testing usually occurs pertaining to a math test taken by pupils in the classroom. Alternate forms information reliability also may be shown in the Manual of the test being taken (See National Council Teachers of Mathematics, 1989).

Most standardized test items contain multiple choice test items and this type may also be used by the teacher when he/she writes a math test. Teacher written math tests are very valuable because they may be taken by pupils throughout the school year whereas standardized tests are generally given once a year. Highly valid tests may be written covering what has been taught in a math unit of study. Thus whatever has been taught and is vital may be included in a math test. Face validity is then used. Multiple choice test items in math need to:

- possess four distractors that are plausible. If three alone are plausible, more chances for guessing the correct response occur.
- distractors should be of equivalent length so that no clues are given for the correct answer.
- correct responses should alternate among the different multiple choice test items so that no patterns are seen as to correct answers.
- have stems which are grammatically correct with each distractor (Ediger, 2007).

Results from pupils' tests provide feedback to both learners and teachers in terms of what needs more emphasis in the mathematics curriculum. True/false test items, clearly written, have merit if the pupil needs to correct the incorrect part. This avoids the fifty percent chance of guessing an answer correctly.

Essay tests may do a good job of evaluating achievement in mathematics if the questions are:

- valid and reliable. Use of quality rubrics increases judging pupil's responses more reliably.
- delimited and stress problem solving, not rote learning.
- written in emphasizing higher levels of cognition such as critical and creative thinking (Ediger, 2006).

Test results then provide information for making lesson and unit decisions in teaching mathematics. Feedback to both pupils and teachers should aid in providing quality objectives, learning opportunities and appraisal procedures in teaching mathematics.

Constructivism in the Mathematics Curriculum

Somewhat opposite of data driven instruction is constructivism. Constructivists (Vygotsky, 1978) greatly minimize the use of tests to ascertain pupil achievement and progress. Teacher observation on a continual basis is used to assist learners in mathematics. Jean Piaget emphasized an individualized approach in using constructivism as a psychology of learning whereas Len Vygotsky stressed the use of small group endeavors. Thus the math teacher observes when and where pupils need help. The assistance generally is not given in terms of an explanation or lecture, but rather questions are raised by the teacher leading the pupil to arrive at correct answers. The math teacher has a thorough grasp of subject matter in assisting pupils to come up with what is accurate. The processes and answers are equally salient in mathematics. If word problems are being stressed, the teacher assists pupils in determining unrecognized words by:

* helping the pupil use context clues in correctly identifying a word.
* using phonics in identifying the initial consonant of a word and then notching sequential letters with corresponding sounds.
* divide an unknown word into syllables, prefixes/ suffixes, and noticing a shorter word within the longer word (Ediger, 2009).

The above listed asterisked items are utilized to recognize an unknown word and then to attach meaning to subject matter read. They are not used, for example, to emphasize learning phonics for its own sake, but used to attach meaning to mathematical subject matter being read.

Constructivism emphasizes that pupils appraise their own individual progress with teacher assistance. Learning is sequential in the minds of pupils, not in the mind of the teacher. The pupil orders new experiences which are directly related to previously learned content. The following kinds of learning opportunities provide pupils with activities to sequence their very own subject matter and skills with mathematics teacher guidance:

* problem solving which stresses deliberation and intrinsic effort.
* project methods stressing construction of objects and items.
* making of geometrical models (Dewey, 1916).

In each of the above asterisked items, the learning experience moves for ward without specific objectives for each facet and stage of achievement. Mistakes are made along the way and are rectified by learners in context, not as separate items to be tested. The teacher of mathematics is there to guide, motivate and encourage, in authentic learnings, but not to tell pupils how to proceed. He/she may model an authentic task prior to learners being actively engaged. Modeling is done to clarify task engagement to pupils. Learning by discovery is a key point to emphasize in constructivist thinking.

REFERENCES

Dewey, John (1916), *Democracy and Education*. New York: Macmillan Company.

Ediger, Marlow (1989), "Psychology of Teaching Mathematics," (1989), *Delta K*, 27 (4), 20-23.

Ediger, Marlow (2006), "Writing in the Mathematics Curriculum," *Journal of Instructional Psychology*, 33 (1), 120-123.

Ediger, Marlow (2007), "Readiness for Mathematics Learning and the Student," *Experiments in Education*, 35 (8), 1-5.

Ediger, Marlow (2009), "For an Effective Reading Program," *Reading Improvement*, 46 (3), 119-122.

National Council Teachers of Mathematics (1989), *Curriculum and Evaluation Standards for School Mathematics*. Reston, Va.: NCTM.

Newton, Xiaoxia (2007), "Reflections of Mathematics Reform," *Phi Delta Kappan*, 27 (4), 20-23.

Vygotsky, Len (1978), *Mind in Society: The Development of Higher Psychological Processes*. Cambridge, Massachusets: Harvard University Press.

Daily Assessment in Ongoing Mathematics Lessons

Too frequently evaluation is equated with standardized testing and yearly evaluations. Thus, testing only and doing this once a year seemingly are adequate. But, there are a plethora of other procedures of evaluation, and on a daily basis, are available and should be utilized. University schools of teacher education need to offer within course work, pertaining to the teaching of mathematics, knowledge and skills emphasizing teacher observation in daily lesson observations. In pre-service programs, university students in teacher education should practice observing and assisting pupils in the classroom setting. There are numerous observations which may be made of the kinds of errors pupils make in mathematics. These must be analyzed collaboratively, or with the class as a whole, in the public school or university classroom. The professor needs to assist university students to notice common errors made and then stress the saliency of assisting pupils to overcome these problematic areas.

Teaching and Learning Situations in Mathematics

Developing interest within pupils for achieving objectives of instruction might well make for a sequential curriculum. Thus, interest propels learners to progress orderly. As seamlessly as possible should be an end result in making connections between the new and the previous learnings acquired by learners. Pupils interest will assist in making it this way. Thus, the mathematics teacher must be certain that each pupil has an adequate fund of knowledge to benefit from the ensuing presentation. Through discussions of what has been presented previously, either inductively or deductively depending upon the learning style inherent, the teacher may notice if pupils benefit from the new subject matter. This is followed with synthesizing the two. The teacher must notice if each learner understands what is being taught and this can be observed if the level of application has been achieved. Being able to apply indicates meaningful learnings. It is unfortunate if a pupil attempts to memorize content for a test and therein fails to apply what should have been achieved for utilization in school and in society (Ediger and Rao, 2011). Higher levels of thinking need to be part of the equation in teaching mathematics. Thus, critical thought is involved when solving word problems. What is needed for the solution is separated from that which is unrelated. This may be quite complex, for instance, when pupils are solving multi-step word problems. Sometimes, a mathematics textbook might stress an unnecessary numeral in a word problem and the pupil is to sort out what is necessary from that being frivolous. In addition to critical thinking, the pupils should have ample opportunities to make creative discoveries. A learner may then discover a different algorithm to arrive at/an answer(s) to column addition or to a practical problem involving quantity and number. Creative and critical thought are needed in CCSS mathematics program.

Pupils should also evaluate themselves individually and collaboratively in working toward higher achievement levels in mathematics. With self evaluation, the learner might well notice specific errors in computation, errors in sequence, process errors, as well as product errors.

Each pupil is important and must achieve well on a daily basis in order to make progress toward more complex objectives of instruction.

REFERENCE

Ediger, Marlow and D. Bhaskara Rao (2011), *Essays in Teaching Mathematics*. New Delhi, India: Discovery Publishing House Ltd.

Factors that Assist Mathematics Achievement

There are selected factors which might well help pupil achievement in mathematics. These need to be studied, and analyzed and conclusions realized. Public schools need to possess a special place where quality video tapes, teaching mathematics journals and university level mathematics education textbooks, internet and web sources are available to acquire relevant knowledge and skills to use in ongoing units of study in the classroom. The psychology of learning, among other factors, must be stressed in teaching and learning situations in order to optimize achievement and progress in mathematics. Thus, pupils need to connect subject to the self, to experiences in society and to the school setting.

Class Size and Learner Progress

How might a class be organized so that pupils may benefit from instruction? This appears to be a perennial question. Hopefully, class size will not. exceed approximately, 20-25 pupils. This should make it possible to teach all pupils effectively.

Pupils may be taught in large group instruction. To initiate a new mathematical unit of study, the teacher must use teaching materials which are clearly visible to all in the classroom. Needed materials of teaching may include a large place value chart with paper strips to show ones, tens, hundreds and thousands values, as well as congruent objects to be used as markers indicating place value. The mathematics teacher may then demonstrate to pupils how to regroup and rename in addition and subtraction. He/she observes pupils carefully to notice that each is listening carefully and noticing how this is done. The learnings are paced and sequential so that learners individually have opportunities to acquire facts, concepts and generalizations necessary to perform these operations successfully. The mathematics teacher observes pupils carefully to notice engagement as each attends, watches, and notices poignant learnings.

Next, the teacher divides pupils into groups of four. These may be heterogeneous or homogeneous depending upon the purpose involved. Each set of four receives a sheet of problems and a smaller place value chart to practice the objectives emphasized in the larger group. The teacher circulates among the committees to notice time on task behaviors as well as meanings pupils attach to place value. Interests of pupils is noticed within each small group and the quality of interactions is also observed. The teacher then carefully monitors achievement to notice what pupils do not understand with assistance given as needed to overcome problem areas. However, it is good to have pupils ponder and discuss indepth necessary ideas in regrouping and renaming. Selected pupils learn best in social situations whereby ideas circulate within a small group of learners.The mathematics teacher records and dates problem areas as well as progress made by pupils using anecdotal approaches.

Cooperative teaching may also be used whereby involved teachers work together to plan sequential lessons. Here, teachers take turns in teaching the large group made up of two or three classrooms of children. This makes inservice education more readily available in that teachers may observe each other teach and offer comments for improvement. Smaller groupings of four or five pupils might then work on problems subsequent to large group instruction. Cooperating teachers might then circulate among committees to offer assistance as needed to foster learner interest and meaning in the ongoing activity.

Individual needs must be met, based on the large and small group endeavors. It is good to document needs of pupils which were noticed in the previous grouping arrangements. Each anecdotal statement then is dated per pupil and necessary help given as listed. The mathematics teacher needs to have needed indepth subject matter and pedagogy in mind in order to offer quality guidance. Mastery learning is salient. Pupils individually must attain sequentially. What is not understood needs remedying so that a solid foundation is built for acquiring ensuing mathematical facts, concepts, and generalizations. Too frequently, the teacher has hurried and moved rapidly to cover content in the basal textbook with little attention paid to learner achievement of each step of progress in an ongoing unit of study.

Inservice Growth

Mathematics teachers must possess the needed knowledge to implement high quality strategies of instruction. Growth and achievement is ongoing in teaching. Thus, the public school should have a convenient place for mathematics teachers to study and converse with colleagues on mathematics content and effective means of instruction. In this area for study, there should be recent mathematics journals, yearbooks and paperbacks published by the National Council Teachers of Mathematics, among others. Encouragement must be given by school administrators for teachers to read and implement ideas which meet standards of quality. The same would be true for housing university level mathematical teacher education texts.

Math teachers may meet together to analyze content and pedagogical methods to improve the curriculum. The dates for meetings and the math literature or topics to be discussed need to be agreed upon. Teachers, also, must elaborate on what has worked well for them pertaining to that used in teaching and learning situations in ongoing lessons and units of study. The doors of effective communication need to be opened among teachers so that good ideas circulate among group members. Trust and consideration for each other is vital. Mathematics teachers and pupils are poignant in the total educational enterprise. Thus, the processes of group work need emphasis. Each can learn much from others and motivate cooperative endeavors. Enthusiasm for learning might well be a motivator to build morale among committee members. New ideas be that motivator to increase energy levels for teaching mathematics!

Mathematics teachers need to engage in self-reflection in which they:

- rehearse what was achieved previously in teaching pupils in noticing that which may be done differently to optimize progress.
- take careful notice of what is needed personally in inservice education to improve teaching performance.
- become increasingly proficient in managing grouping procedures as well as learner behaviour.
- must think in terms of continuous improvement of the self as well as of pupils in mathematical content and skills.

Teachers of mathematics need to develop favorable attitudes in curriculum endeavors. A good self concept must be attained. Thus, self efficacy is a salient goal in that:

- teachers feel competent in teaching pupils of a variety of achievement and ability levels.
- the latest technology can be used very effectively to enhance pupil learning.
- they can provide, fully, for individual differences among learners including children of poverty and from diverse cultures.
- teaching methods can be used which are beneficial to all English Language Learners (ELL) regardless of language proficiency.
- definite provisions can be made to teach diverse categories of handicapped pupils.
- mathematics teachers exhibit pride in their profession when communicating with others.

Mathematics may be integrated with other academic areas, for example, such as the social studies in that learners study Egyptian and Roman systems of numeration and in science whereby mathematics is the language of the physical sciences as in force, distance and work performed given in numerical terms. Integration is stressed when there is a need to do so and it assists pupils to understand relevant facts, concepts, and generalizations.

Evaluation of Achievement

There are selected methods of achievement which need to be used to assess learner progress. Mandated testing occurs once a year and involves the use of standardized tests. Thus, pupils for any grade level have the same directions, time limits and the same scoring key used in computerized scoring. Validity and reliability data is given in the Manual for each test taken by pupils in the pilot study. The mathematics teacher's pupils score from test results is then compared with those in the Manual to ascertain percentile ranking and/or grade equivalent. Numerical data is then obtained to learn about each pupil's achievement as well as average achievement for a classroom and/or school system. From all testing situations, the teacher needs to use printouts/feedback to notice what needs more emphasis. Errors made by pupils stress the need for remedial work in terms of processes and products. Standardized tests are generally given once a school year; thus, in the mean time, teacher made tests also play a vital role in instruction.

Teacher written tests may also include multiple choice test items whereby the stem with one distractor of four given is correct. However, teacher written tests should include essay items; these include problem solving which broadens pupil's knowledge and skills by having authentic word problems to solve. Here, pupils need to show their work in arriving at the correct answer. The advantages of having pupils show processes include the following:

- the teacher may notice thought processes involved by pupils and thus aid is provided to assist pupils in remediation.

- he/she may notice algorithms used by pupils in problem solving.
- reading difficulties in solving word problems.
- incorrect copying of numerals making for errors.
- illegible handwriting making for difficulties to track pupil progress in doing problem solving.

Teacher observation using quality standards of evaluation of pupil work in ongoing lessons, on a daily basis stresses:

- the importance of assisting pupils when difficulties arise in computation and problem solving. With assistance, adequate time must be given for pupils to analyze, synthesize and evaluate, to become self sufficient in remedying difficulties.
- noticing difficulties in individual learner processes to stress remediation in large and small group sessions.

In conclusion

The mathematics curriculum continues to change in terms of subject matter emphasis and methodology in teaching. Quality inservice education is needed to stress the best of objectives for pupil attainment, means for learners to attain these objectives, and appraisal techniques. Education is ongoing and subject to continuous change. Thus, there will always be a need for continuous education.

Teaching Mathematics in the Common Core

The Common Core State Standards (CCSS) has acquired considerable momentum, having been adopted in most states in the union. In contrast, The No Child Left Behind (NCLB) Was Passed into Law in 2002 and has received a plethora of complaints, especially from teachers and school administrators. The complaint rests largely upon the Adequate Yearly Progress (AYP) standards whereby pupils were to measure "proficient" by 2014. Numerous schools have been exempted from this standard, but they must show an alternate way of indicating learner progress. The NCLB section pertaining to pupils being required to pass grade level tests in order to be promoted in grades three through eight is still in vogue as is the requirement for all high school students to pass an exit test to receive a high school diploma (Ediger and Rao, 2011).

The NCLB has numerous weaknesses in the teaching of mathematics. Among others, these include the following:

- it is centred on teaching toward ends, reacher than also including salient processes needed in problem solving.
- it is based on pupils selecting the correct answer from a series of multiple choice test items, making it factual in nature instead of branching out with creative and critical thinking.
- it does not emphasize adequately, the structure of mathematical knowledge, key ideas in understanding subject matter in mathematics.

Common Core State Standards

The CCSS will and should emphasize a complete understanding by teachers and school administrators of its objectives and means of testing and measuring. Thus, each school must have a series of well planned workshops whereby each participant becomes highly knowledgeable about the implementation of CCSS. How CCSS is different and how it resembles previous plans of teaching must be clarified in a meaningful manner. A hands on approach stresses the importance of trying out and reporting back to respective committees results of CCSS attempts in the classroom.

The objectives, here, need to be well understood in depth as well as be meaningful. Learning opportunities to achieve these stated objectives must be discussed in order that individual differences in mathematics receive adequate attention. Understanding of subject matter within these objectives needs to be sequential whereby the learner moves from the known to the unknown. Collaborative and individual endeavors must be in the offing to meet learning styles of individual learners. Inductive and deductive methods alternate the way pupils learn and might well assist each learner to attain as optimally as possible. Concrete, semiconcrete and abstract sequences in achievement guide learners to achieve as well as abilities and skills permit. The focal point is upon the pupil and his/her present level of achievement with indepth attention being given to the mathematical objectives of CCSS. Outcomes, here, preclude developing high quality attitudes in being positive toward and liking mathematics as an academic discipline (Ediger and Rao, 2008).

The psychology of education needs to be emphasized in all mathematical teaching and learning experiences. By incorporating these into ongoing experiences, the pupil has a more optimal opportunity to optimize achievement in ongoing units of study. Thus, pupils need to be given immediate assistance, if possible, to correct that which is incorrect. Pupil interest must be encouraged; motivating learners is important with appropriate readiness activities in order to benefit from the ensuing learnings. If pupils can be aided to perceive purpose in learning, they will tend to sense relevance and utilization of subject matter to be acquired.

Evaluation of Progress

Valid and reliable sources must be utilized in the assessment process including, of course, CCSS testing and measurement. Additional procedures involve the following evaluative procedures:

- objective teacher observation in terms of recommended criteria. This procedure may be used continually as the teacher monitors learner progress. He/she may notice an incorrect response or process used by a pupil and then provide immediate assistance.
- anecdotal statements, dated and recorded for each pupil observed on a random basis.
- behavioral journal kept by the teacher to record in diary entry form progress and achievement of learners.
- portfolios kept by each pupil to save sequential math products of pupils to indicate progress.

REFERENCES

Ediger, Marlow and D. Bhaskara Rao (2009), *Teaching Mathematics in the Elementary School*. New Delhi, India: Discovery Publishing House Ltd.

Ediger, Marlow and D. Bhaskara Rao (2011), *Essays in Teaching Mathematics*. New Delhi, India: Discovery Publishing House.

Mathematics, the Teacher and the Learner

The importance of mathematics in the school curriculum has a long history. During ancient times and during the middle Ages, the quadrivium consisted of geometry and arithmetic, along with astronomy and music. The quadrivium together with the trivium (grammar, rhetoric and logic) made up the Seven Liberal Arts. Textbooks were almost in non-existence and the Master Teacher provided the content to students, who in return, copied down what was imparted. Memorization was a major way of learning content and in this way students revealed achievement.

Grammar, rhetoric (public speaking), as well as logic were inherent in attempts at communicating ideas correctly, and thus being useful in geometry and arithmetic, the latter two academic areas provide the basis for this manuscript (Ediger and Rao, 2011).

Since that time, the mathematics curriculum has gone through a plethora of major revisions, such as modern school mathematics during the 1960s, as well as No Child Left Behind (NCLB) during the first decade of the 21st century. Presently the Common Core State Standards (CCSS) coming into relevance.

The Common Core State Standards (CCSS)

The CCSS provide objectives for kindergarten through college/university levels of school and are to prepare students for higher education or the world of work. Structural ideas are an important basis for selecting relevant subject matter in the school mathematics curriculum. These provide a foundation for understanding key ideas in each lesson/unit taught. To achieve the structure of mathematical content, the teacher needs to utilize recommended methods of instruction which foster learner growth, progress and acquisition of vital concepts and generalizations.

Pupil interest is a must in learning, and the teacher needs to devise strategies which will involve all learners in a lesson presentation. A variety of activities need to be in the offing so that pupils refrain from being bored in learning as well as aiding in providing for individual differences. Thus, the new activities motivate learners to achieve objectives of instruction. Ensuing content taught must be based on the present achievement level of individual pupils. Thus, proper sequence might well be emphasized. Jumping too far ahead of where learners are presently in achievement or repeating unnecessarily what pupils already know wastes time in teaching and learning situations. Seamlessly, pupils need to move forward when connections are made between the new and the old content. This provides readiness for mastery of the new objectives of instruction.

Meaning must be established by the learner in analyzing ensuing subject matter. Thus, understanding of mathematical content is of utmost importance before and during the time new subject matter is presented. In analyzing content pertaining to solving a word problem, the pupil needs to separate what is salient from that which is unnecessary.

Learning opportunities may involve the following, among others, in assisting each learner to achieve well:

- good teaching from carefully chosen basal textbooks, supplementary texts, and workbooks.
- use of teacher made materials such as place value charts, geoboards, counters, fraction charts, hundred boards, drawings and games, among others.

- audio-visual aids, power point learnings, computerized presentations and the white board, as well as utilization of other technology including large group/small group collaborative learning and individual endeavors.
- aid in development of good attitudes toward mathematics, classmates and the larger school population, as well as the total curriculum.

Mathematics teachers must achieve feelings of self-adequacy. Here, the teacher needs to do much reading of professional materials, talk to other teachers about improving the curriculum, attend workshops and conventions on mathematics instruction, as well as take course work on a college/university campuses leading to a graduate degree. There is much that can be done locally for mathematics teachers to become increasingly proficient in teaching. These teachers may schedule a series of meetings whereby problems in teaching are discussed. New procedures discussed may be tried out in class with teaching results elaborated among participants. Newly approved ideas need thorough consideration and implemented on a trial basis. Do they work out well?

Conclusion

Well prepared mathematics teachers in subject matter knowledge is needed in order to diagnose and provide remedial assistance to pupils. They also must be able to develop a high quality curriculum which enhances and stimulates learning. Each pupil needs to achieve as optimally as possible in daily work as well as on standardized tests in mathematics. A final test of learning accrues when pupils are proficient in every day utilization of mathematics.

REFERENCE

Ediger, Marlow, D. Bhaskara Rao (2011), *Essays on Teaching Mathematics*. New Delhi, India: Discovery Publishing House Ltd.

Index